HILARY KEATING

The Flavour
of
HOLLAND

Sketches & Recipes

Schuyt & Co

Dedicated to our husbands Bill and Jacques, and our families
who have lived through this project.

Acknowledgements: Carolyn Gelderman who brought us together, and to
Winnifred Sarre, Cathy Loubser, Ellen Kruimer, Ann Thal Larsen, Tom van Staveren,
Chris Nugteren, Anneke Riel, Gré Langeveld;
Christine Grit (Suikerstichting Nederland),
Liesbeth Boekestein (Centraal Bureau van de Tuinbouwveilingen),
Nataša Krivokuća (Voorlichtingsbureau Vlees)
and Adriaan Peek (Cacao de Zaan).

Using the Recipes

- All conversions are approximate. They have been rounded off to the nearest convenient measure.
- As ovens and pans differ, check and adjust temperatures and timings to conform to your own equipment.
- All spoon measurements used are level unless stated otherwise.
- Use only one of the three measuring systems for a given recipe (either metric or imperial or cup). Do not mix them up.
- All recipes serve 4 to 6 persons unless otherwise indicated.

© 1995 Schuyt & Co, Uitgevers
en importeurs BV, Haarlem
Illustrations by Kirsten Dettor
Photographs by Hilary Keatinge
Graphic design by Volken Beck
Reprinted in 1996
ISBN 90 6097 370 4 NUGI 421/672 CIP

Contents

Introduction

Take two enthusiasts, one Dutch and one Irish, throw them together and something is bound to happen; and it has.

A mutual friend introduced me to Anneke three years ago; we both had ideas about a book, but each felt unable to proceed alone, Anneke was not sure that her English was up to it, and I was quite sure that my `on-the-run' type of cooking was far from professional . We do however have a lot in common, we have both travelled a lot, we are both interested in our own kitchens and those of other nationalities; we both love books – particularly cookery books. We quickly learned about our shared interests and our differences; the ingredients were there – the project was launched.

The book runs on parallel lines, the Dutch at home with their traditions and customs as observed by an outsider – that's me, and the Dutch kitchen, its background and potential from Anneke, the dedicated local.

Holland, aptly known as the Low Countries, but officially called The Netherlands, is a place of long flat landscapes, church spires and water, so much water; and most important of all, so much growing. It seems to the visitor that every square centimetre is under cultivation, and as there are no hedgerows, just ribbons of ditches and canals, it is all visible. There are acres of productive green, a neat patchwork of pasture and furrowed field, while behind the tall poplar screens are lines of man-high trees heavy with fruit.

This country has been a centre for the distribution of produce for centuries; plane, ship and truck loads of goods, local and foreign, pass through the system each day. No other country in the world exports horticultural products to as many places; none is better placed to make the best use of the riches of the agricultural world than The Netherlands.

The cities, towns and villages are steeped in cultural traditions and are so easily accessible – nowhere is much more than an hour and a bit away and it is a joy travelling through the country. For my part, I hope to bring you something of the flavour of life and living in The Netherlands.

The culinary traditions of the country are simple, people here have indeed eaten plain food but what the critics ignore is that in this land of plenty the basics are of excellent quality. Times too are changing, and the modern Dutch cook is being tempted by the media and foreign travel to try new methods and ingredients as well as giving those well tried staples a new and more exciting twist. There is a renewed pride in the traditional wholesomeness of grandmother's era, as well as a willingness to experiment with the new. All that is needed is someone to dispel the myths and show what can be achieved – this has been Anneke's mission.

Come on a journey through a year in The Netherlands, the progress of the book is as seasonal as possible. There is a part to read at leisure, and a part to work from. There are twelve chapters, each representing a month of the year; each chapter begins with a sketch which is historical or factual (or just whimsical). Then follow the recipes, some traditional, most modern, all practically explained and laid out for today's busy cooks. Where relevant, there are additional notes on produce and procedures, many prompted by my queries to Anneke for simple explanations for her specialist use of ingredients and methods.

We have written this book for all newcomers to The Netherlands who seek to understand and to integrate into what for them is a new culture; it is for visitors who would like to take a flavour of the country away when they leave and for adventurous locals who are interested in their own history and culinary traditions. It is a workbook, a present, a souvenir, a book just to read. It is for people like Anneke and myself who have a passion for cookbooks and cookery of all kinds.

Old Year – New Year

Traditions and customs
A part of the Dutch jaarwisseling *– turn of the year*

We begin our journey through twelve months in The Netherlands on the eve of a new year, the last day of December. The Dutch call it *oudejaarsavond* – the evening of the old year, seeing it, initially, as a conclusion rather than a beginning. But then to other time-keepers like myself, the Dutch do tend to look at the passage of time back-to-front: *half twaalf,* for instance, means half before twelve or eleven-thirty, and talk of *eenendertig december* is but the thirty-first.

And so, on this the last day of the year, though it is not a Public Holiday, you will find many public places shut early, even the seemingly ever-open cafés and restaurants switch on the 'closed' sign and most people head for home. As the year draws to an end, the Dutch like to be with their families as they take time to look back nostalgically over what has been, or might have been. One should, they will tell you, square with the past before embracing the new.

Family meals are relaxed as everyone gathers, nothing too formal is served. A number of sweet things feature: *appelflappen* and *appelbeignets,* which are crispy apple turnovers and fried apple puffs respectively; while among the youngsters there is inevitably a competition to see who can eat the most *oliebollen,* these are a kind of deep fried doughnut, but without the hole in the middle.

Frying the *oliebollen* has traditionally been 'man's work', perhaps because in some households they are cooked outside in the open to minimize that all pervasive smell of hot smoky oil. It is a job the lady of the house is glad to relinquish, for it is after all deep midwinter!

Inside, out of the cold, family games are the order of the day. Then, as the evening moves on, television becomes the centre of attention and there have been generations of followers for the satirical review of the Dutch year, *De Oudejaarsavond Conference*. Traditionally this one-man show takes the nationwide audience through the last hour and a half of the passing year.

The tension mounts as the hands of the clock approach the year's demise, when everyone, but it seems everyone, spills out into the night, onto street corners, around town squares, along sleepy canals, all heavily muffled against the cold... expectant... whispering in close-knit groups...

At the stroke of twelve it happens... something uniquely Dutch... hundreds of thousands of fireworks lighten the darkness with trails of amazing brightness, Chinese crackers ricochet along the pavements like the very demons they are supposed to dispel, the buildings rebound with the echo of explosions as the church bells struggle to be heard above the din. What ghost from the year past would dare to remain in that deafening noise? All signs of nostalgia are dispersed as the whiff of gunpowder and its attendant smoke envelops the revellers in eerie swirling shrouds. A celebration to the new year has begun and the bangs and whizzes will reverberate well into the next day.

The atmosphere on the streets is good humoured and very special as friends, neighbours and strangers alike, wish each other *gelukkig nieuwjaar*, Happy New Year.

Champagne corks pop and a late night buffet is served. It is a cold repast, for no one has time for cooking on such a night. The centre piece is the traditional *huzarensalade* – a special Dutch salad which is akin to a potato or Russian salad. There are also platters of pâtés and cheeses and crusty bread; and for those still hungry, there must be at least one more *oliebol* or *appelflap* to be finished off!

New Year's Day sees the wider family paying visits; there are plates of raisin bread and perhaps slices of the famous *duivekater*, a sweet yeast loaf (*see recipe which follows for more about this bread). There are many regional specialities for New Year's Day, mostly waffles, breads and biscuits, and yet again apple puffs or fritters.

Do not miss the significance of the seasonal *oublie* – this thin wafery biscuit, its ends often dipped in chocolate, has been rolled specially to symbolize the hidden mysteries which lie in wait in the year ahead.

'De koffie is altijd klaar' – strong fresh coffee is 'always ready' for visitors whatever the time of day or year, and small cups of it are usually drunk sweet and black with perhaps a drop or two of *koffiemelk*, which is evaporated rather than fresh milk. You may hear a local ask for *'een wolkje alstu'*, puzzling to the outsider until you realize that the 'little cloud' in question is: 'Just a drop or two of milk if it would please you'.

It is not only coffee which will warm the arriving guests, there may be small glasses of *advocaat*. This Dutch speciality is said to have had its origins in an avocado/alcohol mixture favoured by the East Indian traders, but today the basis is brandy, thickened with eggs, sweetened with sugar and often served with a dollop of thick cream on top – in fact it is not drunk at all, but eaten with a spoon. *Advocaat* is used to flavour many desserts and cakes and a thinner version of the drink has found a niche in the export market.

Another favourite tipple during the festive season is a glass of *boerenjongens,* – farmers' boys, brandy with plump marinated raisins; there is also a female variety, *boerenmeisjes,* with apricots. And if drinking raisins and apricots is too much of a challenge, well, they both make excellent toppings for ice-cream.

And finally, after all the excitement and the visiting and the making of serious resolutions, many Dutch households will relax with a traditional evening meal, a New Year's *stamppot,* made of mashed potatoes and vegetables; in some kitchens you will even find it being cooked in the now empty *oliebollenpan* – only the Dutch could think of an effortless way to clean that oily pot!

The New Year Specials

~

We do not give you a complete menu for January, but rather a selection of the seasonal 'musts'. One can not celebrate the New Year in the Netherlands without *oliebollen* and *appelflappen*, though if you live here it is all too easy to buy these freshly made at just about every bakery and street stall.

No Dutch housewife will omit *huzarensalade* from the late night feast, but we also include Anneke's elegant recipe for a halibut mousse which you could add to the midnight buffet. To round off the festivities on New Year's Day, prepare this lentil soup which is a different, easy and substantial one-pot meal, just serve it piping hot with a crusty loaf or two.

Oliebollen – Deep Fried Fritters

Appelflappen – Apple Puffs
(these are eaten at any time, all the time… during the festivities!)

~

Huzarensalade – Dutch Potato Salad

Heilbotmousse met Gerookte Heilbot en Tomatensaus
Mousse of Halibut with Smoked Halibut and Tomato Sauce
(to serve as part of the after-midnight buffet supper)

~

Duivekater – A Sweet Festive Bread

Soesjes – Cream Puffs

Slemp – Saffron milk
(to offer on New Year's Day)

~

Linzensoep – Lentil Soup

Oliebollen – Deep Fried Fritters

The recipe given here is the traditional one; for a change however you could add preserved ginger or pineapple, or even chopped fresh apple to the dried fruit. To save time, make the batter the evening before it is needed. These quantities should make about twenty fritters which sounds a lot but... be warned... in some Dutch families you have to cater for about ten *oliebollen* per person!

INGREDIENTS *for approximately 20 fritters*

75 g (2 ½ oz; ½ cup) **currants**
75 g (2 ½ oz; ½ cup) **raisins**
15 g (½ oz) **baker's yeast or 1 tsp. dried yeast**
1 tsp. **sugar**
150 ml (5 fl.oz; ½ cup + 2 tbsp.) **milk**
250 g (8 oz; 1 ⅔ cup) **plain flour**
½ tsp. **salt**
1 tsp. **grated lemon zest**
2 **eggs**
1 lt (2 pts; 1 qt) **vegetable oil for deepfrying**

PREPARATION

• Wash and dry the currants and raisins.
• Dissolve the yeast and sugar in the milk.
• Sieve the flour and salt into a bowl, mix in the lemon zest. Make a well in the middle, add the dissolved yeast mixture and work into a third of the flour.
• Lightly beat the eggs and add to the bowl.
• Using a wooden spoon, beat vigorously until all these ingredients form a smooth batter.
• Mix in the fruit.
• Cover and leave in a warm place until the batter has doubled in volume, or overnight in a cool place.
• Heat the oil in a deep pan until very hot (190°C / 375°F).
• Using a ladle dipped in the hot oil (or an ice-cream scoop), lift spoonfuls of the dough – each about the size of an egg, and drop into the hot fat. Fry for about 5 minutes, turning as necessary, until

a deep golden colour on all sides. Do not fry too many at a time, as it is important that the temperature of the oil remains constant to avoid the *oliebollen* becoming greasy.
- Drain on kitchen paper.

PRESENTATION
- Dust the *oliebollen* with icing sugar and serve warm or cold.

Appelflappen – Apple Puffs

For the *appelflappen* Anneke likes to use the Dutch Elstar apple, and she advises that if buying the puff pastry it is best to use that made with butter, rather than margarine. In The Netherlands readymade fresh pastry can be bought by the pound from the baker, or frozen in handy 15 × 15 cm (6 × 6 inch) squares. Be generous in turning the cooked apple turnovers in the sugar mixture, even if this means mixing some extra.

INGREDIENTS *for approximately 15 puffs*
  500 g (1 lb) **puff pastry** (fresh or frozen)
  1 kg (2 lbs) **medium-sized tart apples**
  100 g (3⅓ oz; ½ cup) **sugar**
  2 tsp. cinnamon

PREPARATION
- Preheat the oven to 225°C / 440°F.
- Roll out the (defrosted) pastry to a 3 mm (⅛ inch) thickness. Cut out 15 cm (6 inch) rounds – gathering up the scraps and re-rolling as necessary.
- Peel and core the apples and cut into rings 1½ cm (½ inch) thick.
- Mix the sugar and cinnamon; set aside half of this mixture on a plate.
- Place a slice of apple on a pastry round, put a teaspoonful of the sugar mixture in the middle, dampen the edges and cover with a second round of pastry.
- Put the turnovers on a baking sheet which has been sprinkled with water.

- Bake for about 15 minutes, or until well puffed and golden.

- Remove from the oven and immediately turn the turnovers, one by one, in the reserved sugar mixture.
- Serve warm or at room temperature.

Huzarensalade – Dutch Potato Salad

The *huzarensalade* requires equal quantities of potato, apple and any kind of cold roasted meat. The Dutch housewife does not usually roast joints of meat, she buys what she needs from the butcher or delicatessen. Traditionally the salad is decorated to remind one of time – the salad is moulded to form a clock, halved hard-boiled eggs are arranged to mark the hours, and strips of tomato or beetroot set the hands to midnight.

INGREDIENTS

For the salad
    250 g (½ lb) **waxy potatoes**
    250 g (½ lb) **red skinned apples**
    2 **large gherkins**
    1 **shallot**
    250 g (½ lb) **cold roast pork**

For the dressing
    125 g (¼ lb; ½ cup) **mayonnaise**
    125 g (¼ lb; ½ cup) **thick natural yoghurt**
    1 tbsp. **apple vinegar**
    1 tsp. **smooth mustard**
    1 tsp. **honey**
    salt and freshly ground black pepper

To serve
large bunch of cress or parsley
1 tomato
2 hardboiled eggs (or 6 quails eggs)

PREPARATION

- Peel and dice the potatoes; boil in salted water until just tender. Drain, rinse in cold water and cool.
- Core and dice the apples, chop the gherkins, peel and chop the shallot, mix well to prevent discolouration of the apple.
- Dice the pork.
- Mix the dressing ingredients and add the potatoes, apple mixture and pork.
- Season with salt and pepper.
- Peel and remove the seeds from the tomatoes, cut into strips.
- Hardboil the eggs, plunge into cold water; peel and halve.
- Wash, dry and finely chop cress or parsley.

PRESENTATION

- Mound the potato mixture onto a large platter, and smooth the surface.
- Cover with the chopped cress or parsley.
- Decorate with halved hard-boiled eggs and tomato strips.

Heilbotmousse met Gerookte Heilbot en Tomatensaus
Mousse of Halibut with Smoked Halibut and Tomato Sauce

INGREDIENTS *for a 22-24 cm (9 inch) smooth-sided ring mould*

For the mousse
- 50 g (2 oz; ¼ cup) potato
- 1 shallot
- a clove garlic
- 50 g (2 oz; ¼ cup) leeks
- 25 g (1 oz; 2 tbsp.) butter
- 250 g (½ lb) fillet of fresh halibut
- 2 tbsp. lemon juice
- 1 tsp. powdered gelatine
- salt and freshly ground white pepper
- 125 ml (4 fl oz; ½ cup) cream
- 1 egg white
- 200 g (6 ½ oz) sliced smoked halibut

For the sauce
- 1 large tomato
- 1 tsp. tomato purée
- 1 tbsp. red wine vinegar
- 3 tbsp. oil
- ¼ tsp. cayenne
- salt and freshly ground black pepper

PREPARATION
- Peel and chop the potato, peel and finely chop the shallot and garlic, thinly slice and wash the leek; gently fry these in the butter until soft, about 5 minutes.
- Sprinkle the halibut fillet with the lemon juice, place on the softened vegetables, cover and cook gently for a further 10 minutes or until the fish is just cooked.
- In a small pan sprinkle the gelatine onto a little water, let it stand for 1 minute, then dissolve over a low heat.
- Purée the vegetables and fish together, adding the gelatine and a

little of the cream.
- Season with salt and white pepper; leave to cool.
- Whip the remaining cream until thick.
- Whisk the egg white until stiff and fold into the fish purée with the whipped cream.
- Oil the mould, line with slices of smoked halibut.
- Add the fish purée, cover with foil and chill for at least 3 hours or until set.

- *To make the Tomato Sauce:* Peel and remove seeds from the the tomato and purée with the tomato purée and vinegar. Blend in the oil. Season with cayenne, salt and pepper.

PRESENTATION
- Run a knife round the sides of the mould and turn out onto a platter; spoon a little of the tomato sauce around it.
- Serve the remaining sauce separately.

Duivekater – A Sweet Festive Bread

This sweet bread from North Holland has a name that has long intrigued the historians; one interpretation is that it derives from the French *deux fois quatre*, two times four, for the festive loaf was said to be twice as heavy as an everyday fourpenny bread. It was often baked as a long oblong loaf which the 17th century writers likened to a shinbone. If you study some of Jan Steen's paintings of that era, particularily those of the feast of St. Nicholas, you will see that the *duivekater* features prominently. This bread was traditionally eaten from that saint's day right through to the Feast of the Three Kings on 6th January.

INGREDIENTS

    30 g (1 oz) **baker's yeast or 2 tsp. dried yeast**
    300 ml (10 fl oz; 1 cup + 3 tbsp.) **milk**
    500 g (1 lb; 3 ⅓ cups) **flour**
    50 g (1 ⅔ oz; ¼ cup) **sugar**
    1 tsp. salt
    1 tbsp. grated lemon zest
    25 g (1 oz; 2 tbsp.) **butter**
    1 egg

PREPARATION

- Dissolve the yeast in the milk.
- Sieve the flour into a bowl, make a well in the middle, add the dissolved yeast mixture and work into a third of the flour.
- Add the sugar, salt, lemon zest and butter; knead into a smooth and elastic ball.
- Cover the dough and leave until it has doubled in volume.
- Preheat the oven to 175°C/350°F.
- Punch the air out of the dough and form into an oblong. Make a 5 cm (2 inch) slash in from each end.
- Leave to prove for a further 15 minutes. Make a few diagonal cuts across the top of the loaf.
- Beat the egg with a little water and brush over the loaf.
- Transfer to a greased baking sheet and bake for 20 minutes. Reduce the heat to 150°C/300°F and bake for a further 15 minutes.
- Cool on a wire rack.

PRESENTATION

- Serve cut into thin slices spread with butter.

An important World Première took place on 3rd January, 1638 – *De Gijsbrecht van Amstel*. This theatre piece was written by the famous Dutch writer Joost van den Vondel and it brought to the public, in verse, the story of the founding of the city of Amsterdam. It is a stirring tale filled with devastations, intrigues and killings most foul; this drama used to be performed during the New Year period right up to the end of the nineteen sixties. It is a very long play indeed and it was no wonder that during the interval members of the audience required some diverting fare; for many years it was the tradition to gather in the foyer to discuss the latest production while nibbling minute cream puffs and sipping tiny cups of *slemp* – a spicy milk drink (recipe follows). A revival of the play was staged in January 1995.

Slemp – Saffron Milk

INGREDIENTS *for approximately 15 small cups*
   2 tsp. tea leaves (preferably Indian tea)
   a small piece of lemon zest
   a small piece of cinnamon stick
   a blade of mace
   1 sachet saffron (or ⅛ tsp.)
   2 cloves
   1 lt (2 pts; 1 qt) milk
   40 g (1½ oz; ¼ cup) sugar or to taste
   3 egg yolks (or 1 yolk + 1 tsp. cornflour)
   freshly grated nutmeg

PREPARATION
- Tie the tea leaves, lemon zest and all the spices into a piece of cheese cloth (or use a tea infuser).
- Bring the milk to the boil, remove from the heat; steep the tea and spices in the milk for about an hour.
- Strain the milk into a clean pan, discarding the tea leaves and spices, add sugar to taste.
- Beat the egg yolks (or yolk and cornflour) slightly, add a little of the warm liquid, then pour back into the pan.
- Stirring all the time, heat gently until thickened, but do not boil.

PRESENTATION
- Serve in warmed heat-resistant glasses or cups. Sprinkle a little freshly grated nutmeg on top.

Soesjes – Cream Puffs

Many Dutch bakeries sell these small puff pastries with either a savoury filling (these are popular cocktail snacks, known in Dutch as *hapjes,* which literally translate as 'morsels') or with a sweet filling.

INGREDIENTS *for approximately 40 small puffs*
  100 ml (3 ½ fl oz; a scant ½ cup) **water**
  50 g (1 ⅔ oz; ¼ cup) **butter**
  50 g (1 ⅔ oz; ⅓ cup) **plain flour**
  a pinch of salt
  2 small eggs
  ½ tsp. gelatine
  125 ml (¼ pt; ½ cup) **cream**
  1 tbsp. castor sugar
  icing sugar

PREPARATION
  • Preheat the oven to 225°C / 425°F.
  • Put the water and butter into a saucepan and bring to the boil, cook until the butter has melted.
  • Add the flour and salt all at once, stir continuously until the dough pulls away from the sides of the pan and forms a ball.
  • Take the pan off the heat and beat in the eggs, one at a time until the mixture is smooth and shiny.
  • Using two teaspoons, or a pastry bag with a smooth nozzle, pipe little heaps of dough onto a greased and floured baking sheet.
  • Bake for about 10 minutes, or until puffed and golden.
  • Cool on a wire rack.
  • In a small pan sprinkle the gelatine onto a little water, leave for 1 minute, then dissolve over a low heat.
  • In a bowl beat the cream and sugar until thick, gradually adding the dissolved gelatine.

PRESENTATION
  • Open the puffs with a knife or scissors and fill with the cream.
  • Dust with icing sugar.

Linzensoep – Lentil Soup

INGREDIENTS *for approximately 10 servings*

500 g (1 lb) **brown lentils**
250 g (½ lb; 1 cup) **carrots**
250 g (½ lb; 1½ cups) **onions**
250 g (½ lb; 1 cup) **celery**
100 g (3½ oz) **smoked bacon**
25 g (1 oz; 2 tbsp.) **butter**
1 lt (2 pts; 1 qt) **stock or water**
1 × 450 g (1 lb; 2 cup) **tin/can tomatoes**
1 tbsp. **tomato purée**
salt and freshly ground black pepper
a few sprigs of parsley
100 g (3½ oz; 1 cup) **grated cheese** (mature Gouda)

PREPARATION

- Check the lentils for any grit or other impurities, then rinse.
- Peel the carrots and onions, trim the celery; roughly chop all the vegetables; cut the bacon into small pieces.
- In a deep pan gently fry the vegetables and bacon in the butter until soft.
- Add the prepared lentils, stock, tomatoes and tomato purée.
- Bring to the boil, cover and simmer for about an hour or until the lentils are tender.
- Season with salt and pepper.

PRESENTATION

- Chop the parsley and sprinkle onto the soup.
- Serve the grated cheese separately.

Elfstedentocht and Carnival

Competition on ice in the north; colourful pageant in the south

'...And now the weather forecast for the next 24 hours: High pressure is building over eastern Europe; wind from the south-east force 2-4. Outlook: continuing very cold with a sharp frost.'

At this point most of us hibernating folk will reach for the central-heating controls and pile another log onto the fire. In the Dutch province of Friesland however, this broadcast coming through on a midwinter's day has the opposite effect. Imagine the scene – a weak wintry sun glistens on a frozen canal; a small group of anxious-looking people is gathered on the verge, close to a frosty bridge; they peer down at the ice, look upwards to study the cloud line, debate the wind strength. Suddenly around the corner of the icy road comes a lycra-clad group of athletes in training, they get a 'thumbs up' from our group, one of whom is now boring a measuring pole into the ice; with renewed urgency the runners pound away into the distance. There is a fevered air of expectation wherever you turn; what is it all about?

If and only if, this weather holds for the next week or so, then there is the hope that some 200 kilometres of canal, inland sea and even the great IJssel lake itself, will be safe enough for thousands of pairs of flashing skates to take part in the *Elfstedentocht* – the Eleven Towns Skating Race.

Friesland is one of the oldest provinces of The Netherlands, with evidence of occupation going back to 400 BC. The rich farming lands are set between ribbons of canal and wider waterways which for centuries were the only means of communication for those living on the land. With so much water around it is not surprising that ice-skating is one of Friesland's two particular sports – the other being *Kaatsen*, which is a form of handball.

The characteristics of both landscape and people are noticeably different from other parts of The Netherlands. The farmhouses are distinctive, with their massively sloping roofs which dominate the clusters of windblown trees. The signposts too give evidence of a difference – the *Friese* language, spoken by many locals, old and young, and which is, at its roots, closer to English than Dutch. The fiercely independent Frieslanders, proud of their Nordic heritage, may even offer visitors the opportunity to hold a special Frisian passport.

The more prosperous part of Friesland, Westergo, borders what was once the Zuiderzee, now the landlocked IJsselmeer, and on the northern sea coast the province gives onto the tidal Waddenzee. This whole area was in its heyday in the times of the Hanseatic League, when prosperous 15th century merchants and seamen crowded the towns of Leeuwarden, Dokkum, Franeker, Harlingen, Bolsward, Workum, Hindelopen, Stavoren, Sloten, IJlst and Sneek. Today, these eleven towns are on the course of the world's most famous skating race.

There are reports of such races going back over the centuries; as early as the mid 1700's there were attempted ice marathons throughout Friesland, but it was not until 1890 that the first circuit of a number of towns was timed. Then some years later, in the dawn of Saturday 2nd January, 1909, twenty two participants struggled through atrocious weather to skate out of Leeuwarden; the first official *Elfstedentocht* was under way. Only nine managed to finish that race and the winner had covered the gruelling 194 km course in just under fourteen hours.

As interest in the race grew, it was decided to open the event to those who wanted to take part as endurance rather than speed participants. At the time of the last race (the fourteenth) in 1986 the number of the former was up to 17,000; while of the 340 in the race proper, the fastest speed was down to 6 hours 46 minutes, an average of 28.76 km/h.

The entire province is involved in the *Elfstedentocht*, if not on the ice then in the numerous preparations and support activities. Kluning (crossing) points are laid where the skaters must *klunen* – scramble from one canal to the other or where they have to cross bridges to avoid thin patches of ice; there are kilometres of crowd barriers to be put into place as the entire area becomes jammed with journalists, TV cameras and simply thousands of spectators who pack the province for what must be the world's greatest show on ice. The rest of The Netherlands too grinds to a halt, as everyone wherever they happen to be, sits glued to the commentaries from television and radio.

Along the course, First Aid groups stand at the ready for accidents on the ice or for those struck down by the intense cold; race monitors scribble the numbers and times of the fast moving participants; there are literally dozens of food stalls along the route and on the ice, selling food and drinks; and of course there is a great range of glitzy souvenirs. It is like something straight out of a winter scene depicted by the famous landscape painters Bruegel and Averkamp: groups of chilled spectators huddled round steaming vats waiting for bowls of warming *erwtensoep* – thick split pea soup, some clutching mugs of *anijsmelk*, which is an infusion of aniseed in sweetened milk, while others sip tots of *Beerenburg*. This Frisian geneva (Dutch gin) distilled with herbs and roots, is guaranteed to warm you right down to your toes.

While this spectacle is Friesland's own, south of the great rivers – the Rhine and its tributaries, there is a festivity which takes place annually, hail or shine – February is the time of Carnival. During the run up to the Lenten period of fast and abstinence, the Catholic south has party time. As early as November a Prince is elected in each village and three months later, with much clamour and laughter he leads his colourful procession of costumed locals along the streets by day and through the cafés by night. The most famous parades take place in 's-Hertogenbosch, capital of North Brabant, and Maastricht in the province of Limburg.

No one appears to sleep during the four days before Ash Wednesday and certainly no one seems to work; a farmer's smock, a 'kerchief round your neck and endless energy are the only requirements. The beers will flow freely and every frying pan in the region will be busy cooking endless huge pancakes topped with sizzling bacon and bubbling cheese. The foodstalls of Limburg have *nonnevotten* on sale, these are knots of deep-fried dough dredged with sugar, or maybe, as in Brabant, *worstebroodjes* – sausage rolls with a difference, as bread dough, rather than pastry, is baked round the sausage.

Carnival in the south of The Netherlands is altogether a more friendly affair than in other locations in the world, and safer too than the wild streets of Cologne or Rio, and from experience I know that even as a stranger it is impossible to be there and not to be drawn in to all the fun.

Winter Favourites

⌒

Our modern winter habitat is not such a difficult place to live in and as few of us have to spend hours battling against the elements, we can appreciate some lighter touches to our daily winter fare. Anneke has divided the February recipes into threes: three salads whose basic ingredients are winter vegetables, three very traditional winter dishes and three warming puddings. These last feature on most restaurant menus where Dutch dishes are on offer and while they are included here with other traditional favourites perhaps it would be best to serve them after a main course which is somewhat lighter than these casseroles.

Fruitige Witlofsalade – Fruity Chicory Salad

Bietensalade – Beetroot Salad

Knolselderijsalade – Celeriac Salad

⌒

Erwtensoep – Dutch Pea Soup

Hachee – Beef Stew with Onions

Stamppot met Andijvie en Spekjes
Mashed Potatoes with Escarole and Crispy Fried Bacon

⌒

Rijstebrij met Tutti Frutti
Rice Pudding with Dried Fruit Compote

Griesmeelpudding met Rode Bessesapsaus
Semolina Pudding with Redcurrant Sauce

Trommelkoek – Steamed Fruit Pudding

Fruitige Witlofsalade – Fruity Chicory Salad

Chicory has long been a Dutch staple and is usually eaten hot, each head wrapped in ham and covered in a cheese sauce. In this recipe the uncooked white chicory is combined in a salad with the red-leaved variety and tossed with fruits and nuts. The pomegranate and the grenadine syrup made from it, give this recipe an exotic flavour. The arrival in The Netherlands of many different peoples from the Mediterranean countries has meant that a number of previously unobtainable fruits and vegetables are now widely available and commonly used.

You could use a teaspoon of honey instead of the syrup, and a couple of tablespoonfuls of plumped raisins in place of the pomegranate.

INGREDIENTS

For the salad
>50 g (2 oz; ⅓ cup) shelled walnuts
>250 g (½ lb) chicory
>a small head of radicchio rosso
>1 crisp apple
>1 banana
>1 tsp. lemon juice

For the dressing
>1 tsp. grenadine syrup
>1 tbsp. apple vinegar
>salt and freshly ground black pepper
>a pinch of cayenne
>3 tbsp. sunflower oil

To serve
>1 pomegranate

PREPARATION
- Toast and roughly chop the walnuts.
- Remove any damaged outer leaves and the hard core from the chicory and radicchio; cut into thin slices, rinse and drain.

- Core and chop the apple, peel and slice the banana; sprinkle both with the lemon juice.
- Mix the salad vegetables, nuts and fruits in a large bowl.
- *To make the dressing:* Mix the syrup and vinegar. Season with salt, pepper and cayenne to taste; blend in the oil.

PRESENTATION
- Toss the salad with the dressing 30 minutes before serving.
- Cut through the pomegranate skin and peel off; scoop out the seeds and sprinkle over the salad.

Bietensalade – Beetroot Salad

Oranges and lemons ring the changes in this beetroot recipe; if using raw beetroots they should be cooked with their skins on, for 20-30 minutes depending on their size, then cooled and peeled. *Crème fraîche* is close to sour cream though it has a higher fat content; it is better than sour cream for cooked dishes as it does not curdle as easily. Lamb's lettuce, *(ezelsoor* – which means the ears of a donkey in Dutch, is also called corn salad or by its French name *mâche)*, is basically a winter green and has been popular for years throughout continental Europe in salads, or even lightly sautéed like spinach. It makes an excellent garnish.

INGREDIENTS

For the salad
  2 cooked beetroots
  1 tsp. grated lemon zest
  1 tsp. lemon juice
  1 orange

For the dressing
  a few sprigs of parsley
  1 spring onion
  125 g (4 oz; ½ cup) *crème fraîche*
  125 g (4 oz; ½ cup) thick natural yoghurt
  1 tbsp. lemon juice
  1 tsp. honey
  salt and freshly ground black pepper

To serve
  2 tbsp. sunflower seeds
  100 g (3 oz) lamb's lettuce

PREPARATION

- Peel, then cut the cooked beetroot into julienne; sprinkle with the lemon zest and juice, cover and leave for about an hour.
- Remove peel and pith from the orange and discard. Slice the orange thinly, then quarter each slice.
- Toast the sunflower seeds.
- Rinse and dry the lamb's lettuce
- *To make the dressing:* Wash and chop the parsley, finely slice the spring onion.
- Mix the *crème fraîche*, yoghurt, lemon juice, honey, parsley and spring onion. Season with salt and pepper.

PRESENTATION

- Arrange the lamb's lettuce round a serving platter, form a circle of orange in the middle.
- Just before serving, arrange the beetroot around the orange; sprinkle the whole with the toasted sunflower seeds.

Knolselderijsalade – Celeriac Salad

Knolselderij – celeriac, also known as celery root, celery knob or turnip-rooted celery, is quite a different vegetable from the crunchy green/white stalks we usually associate with the name 'celery', which in The Netherlands is called *bleekselderij*. Celeriac is a root vegetable, and though not very pretty to look at, which may explain its lack of popularity in some countries, it has a rich nutty celery flavour and can be eaten raw or cooked. It makes a good substitute for celery in soups and casseroles. Note the use of yet another type of celery – celery herb in the Dutch pea soup which follows; it is grown in most Dutch herb gardens. The leaf from the regular celery could be used instead.

INGREDIENTS
For the salad
    500 g (1 lb; 2 cups) celeriac
    1 small head of iceberg lettuce
    50 g (2 oz; ⅓ cup) roasted, salted cashew nuts

For the dressing
    1 apple
    1 banana
    2 tbsp. raisins
    1 tsp. curry powder
    1 tsp. lemon juice
    125 g (4 oz; ½ cup) thick natural yoghurt
    salt and freshly ground black pepper

PREPARATION
• Bring a pan of salted water to the boil.
• Peel and coarsely grate the celeriac, add to the boiling water and cook for about 2 minutes.
• Pour off the cooking liquid, rinse the celeriac in cold water, drain and allow to cool.
• Shred and wash the lettuce. Dry. Chop the nuts.

- *To make the dressing:* Core and finely chop the apple, mash the banana; mix both with the raisins, curry powder, lemon juice and yoghurt.
- Season with salt and pepper.

PRESENTATION
- Mix the celeriac and lettuce with the dressing. Sprinkle with the nuts.

Erwtensoep – Dutch Pea Soup

There are probably as many versions of Dutch pea soup as there are people in The Netherlands; Anneke prefers to use pork shoulder for the soup as it is less fatty than the trotters used in her grandmother's day; the carrots give it a sweet flavour, the potatoes supply the body. As there are numerous kinds of smoked sausage it is up to individual taste whether you use pork, beef, a mixture of the two, or your favourite Polish variety. This soup is a meal in itself and needs no further accompaniment other than slices of dark rye bread and *ontbijtspek* or any cured bacon or ham. *Ontbijtspek* is a smoked streaky bacon, sold in wafer thin slices; it can be eaten without any further cooking.

INGREDIENTS
2 lt (4 pts; 2 qts) **water**
500 g (1 lb; 2 ½ cups) **green split peas**
500 g (1 lb) **piece of pork shoulder** (including bone)
1 **bay leaf**
1 tsp. **thyme**
3 **cloves**
250 g (½ lb; 1 cup) **carrots**
200 g (7 oz; 1 ¼ cups) **onions**
250 g (½ lb; 1 cup) **celeriac**
250 g (½ lb; 1 cup) **leeks**
250 g (½ lb) **smoked sausage**
salt and freshly ground black pepper

To serve
    a few sprigs of celery herb
    slices of black rye bread
    mustard
    100 g (¼ lb) Dutch *ontbijtspek* or any thinly sliced cured or
    smoked bacon

PREPARATION

- Put the water, split peas, pork shoulder, bayleaf, thyme and cloves into a large pan and bring to the boil.
- Remove any scum which rises to the surface.
- Cover the pan and stirring occasionally, simmer for 45 minutes or until the peas have cooked to a purée.
- Peel and roughly chop the carrots, onions and celeriac, slice and wash the leeks.
- Lift the pork shoulder out of the soup, cut the meat into small pieces, discard the bone and return the meat to the soup with the smoked sausage (in one piece) and all the vegetables. Cook gently for about 30 minutes.
- Remove and slice the sausage, return to the soup.
- Season with salt and pepper.

PRESENTATION

- Chop the celery herb, sprinkle onto the soup.
- Serve accompanied by thin slices of rye bread spread with a little mustard and topped with *ontbijtspek*.

Note: For the best results make this soup the day before required and leave it partially covered in a cool place.

Hachee – Beaf Stew with Onions

This is a simple casserole with an eastern flavour supplied by the cloves. In The Netherlands, meat is sold almost fat-free, ready sliced or in small pieces. The best beef for stewing is *riblappen*, difficult even to translate, similar to slices of English style rib roast. These slices do have a little fat and give a good meaty gravy. Note that in other Dutch recipes where there is mention of *jus* – it is simply the juice from the cooked meat, to be served as it comes and not thickened as in this casserole.

INGREDIENTS

750 g (1½ lb) **lean stewing beef**
350 g (12 oz; 2 cups) **onions**
25 g (1 oz; 2 tbsp.) **butter**
1 tbsp. vegetable oil
1 tsp. sugar
1 tbsp. flour
250 ml (½ pt; 1 cup) **beef stock/wine or water**
2 bay leaves
2 cloves
2 tbsp. red wine vinegar
salt and freshly ground black pepper

PREPARATION

• Cube the beef and pat dry on paper towel.
• Peel and slice the onions.
• Heat the butter and oil in a large casserole.
• When the butter/oil is hot, brown the meat on all sides. Remove the meat from the pan with a slotted spoon and set aside.
• Add the onions and sugar to the remaining butter in the pan and gently fry until golden.
• Stir in the flour and fry for a few minutes longer until the flour takes on colour.
• Warm the stock and add to the pan together with the beef, bay leaves, cloves and vinegar.
• Season with salt and pepper.
• Bring to the boil, cover and simmer over a very low heat for 2 hours, or until the meat is very tender.

PRESENTATION

• Serve with potatoes and a winter vegetable, such as red cabbage or sprouts.

Stamppot – mashed potatoes and vegetables, a basic Dutch dinner

No book on Dutch cuisine would be complete without *de stamppotten* – the mashed dishes; these are often served as a complete family meal in themselves, or with braised meats as they make a good accompaniment for the gravy. The basic ingredient is a floury potato which is cooked with either a root vegetable, like carrot, or with hardy greens like cabbage or *boerenkool* – curly kale; the vegetables and potatoes are then mashed with butter and seasoning. Finer leafed vegetables like *andijvie* – escarole, or *raapsteeltjes* – turnip tops, do not need cooking but are shredded and simply folded into the hot mashed potato.

Today's cooks, in The Netherlands anyway, are quite spoilt and can buy most vegetables washed and ready chopped from the supermarket or greengrocer. There are good brands of powdered potato purée which mix up in seconds and make these dishes possible even if rushed for time.

Tradition has it that the most famous version of all these mashed dishes – *hutspot* – dates back to October 1574. The Spaniards had laid siege to the city of Leiden for almost a year; the inhabitants were weak and starving when William of Orange craftily flooded all the surrounding countryside. He then ordered his fleet, the famous Sea Beggars under the great admiral Boisot, to advance with the rising waters over the fields. On 1st October, helped by storm winds and a high tide, they inched their way forward and made it right up to the city walls. Two days later they finally routed the oppressors.

William's forces not only saved the city but brought with them desperately needed food supplies: mainly bread and cheese and herring. The story goes on however, that a small boy freed from the beleaguered city went scavenging in the deserted Spanish camp for any edibles left behind and came upon some cooking pots still warm with mashed parsnip, beans and other vegetables – what a find for a starving lad. *Hutspot* takes the place of honour on every table at the liberation festivities still held in Leiden each year on the 3rd October.

In later times, when potato had become the country's staple, it was substituted for the beans, and carrot replaced the parsnip; strangely parsnip is very out of fashion in The Netherlands today and is almost impossible to find here.

Stamppot met Andijvie en Spekjes
Mashed Potatoes with Escarole and Crispy Fried Bacon

Andijvie – escarole, with its fluted leaves is not unlike a lettuce to look at, but it is in fact a member of the chicory family; sometimes referred to as broad or curly leafed endive. It has a slightly bitter taste and is eaten as a salad green, braised, or as in this very typical Dutch recipe.

INGREDIENTS
400 g (¾ lb) escarole
250 g (½ lb) rindless bacon (one thick piece or ready diced)
1 kg (2 lbs) floury potato
25 g (1 oz; 2 tbsp.) butter
milk to mix
salt and freshly ground black pepper

PREPARATION:
• Wash and drain the escarole, shred finely and set aside.
• Dice the bacon and fry until crisp, set aside and reserve the fat.
• Peel and quarter the potatoes and put in a large pan with just enough water to cover. Bring to the boil.
• Cover and cook over a medium heat for about 20 minutes or until the potatoes are cooked.
• Mash the potatoes with any remaining cooking liquid and the butter. Add enough milk to make a soft purée.
• Season with salt and pepper.
• Fold in the escarole, bacon and bacon fat. Return to the heat and warm through.

Rijstebrij met Tutti Frutti
Rice Pudding with Dried Fruit Compote

In Dutch cuisine *tutti frutti* is a selection of whole dried fruits, often sold ready mixed – usually apples, pears, apricots and prunes; it is not the same as the mixture of chopped preserved fruits used in Italian desserts which has the same name. Any combination of dried fruits can be used in this dessert.

Instead of simmering over the heat this pudding could be baked in a slow oven – it will take about an hour.

INGREDIENTS
For the compote
  200 g (7 oz; 1⅓ cups) **mixed dried fruits** (*tutti frutti*)
  1 tbsp. **lemon juice**
  ½ **vanilla pod**
  1 **cinnamon stick**

For the pudding
  75 g (2½ oz; ⅓ cup) **round-grained rice**
  750 ml (1½ pt; 3 cups) **milk**
  a pinch of salt
  ½ **vanilla pod**
  a small piece of **lemon zest**
  2 tbsp. **sugar**
  ½ tsp. **ground cinnamon**

PREPARATION
  • *To make the compote:* Put the dried fruits in a pan with water to cover and leave to soak overnight.
  • Add the lemon juice, vanilla pod and cinnamon stick to the fruits and the soaking liquid.
  • Bring to the boil, cover and simmer for about 30 minutes.
  • Remove both vanilla pod and cinnamon stick.
  • Transfer the compote to a serving bowl, cover and allow to cool.

- *To make the pudding:* Wash the rice in cold running water until the water runs clear, drain.
- Bring the milk to the boil, add the salt, vanilla pod and lemon zest.
- Add the rice and stir until it reaches boiling point again.
- Lower the heat, cover and simmer for about an hour, stirring occasionally.
- Remove the vanilla pod and lemon zest, and stir in the sugar.

PRESENTATION
- Spoon the rice into a bowl or individual dishes.
- Just before serving spoon the *tutti frutti* over the rice and sprinkle with a little ground cinnamon.
- Serve warm or at room temperature.

Griesmeelpudding met Rode Bessesapsaus
Semolina Pudding with Redcurrant Sauce

Unsweetened redcurrant juice is available in The Netherlands in 250 ml (½ pt; 1 cup) bottles, though cranberry or any other red berry juice could be used for this recipe.

There is another famous Dutch dessert made with this juice, it is called *Haagse Bluf* – a concoction of frothy egg whites, redcurrant juice and sugar, which is served with a thin rolled biscuit. History does not reveal exactly why the good citizens of The Hague are considered such 'braggers'! (the dictionary translation of *bluf*).

INGREDIENTS *for a 750 ml (1 ½ pt; 3 cup) pudding mould*
For the pudding
   500 ml (1 pt; 2 cups) **milk**
   50 g (2 oz; ⅓ cup) **semolina**
   1 **egg**
   2 tbsp. **sugar**

For the sauce
  250 ml (½ pt; 1 cup) **unsweetened redcurrant juice**
  2 tbsp. sugar
  ½ cinnamon stick
  1 tsp. potato starch
  3 tbsp. water

PREPARATION

- Bring the milk to the boil.
- Add the semolina, stirring continuously until the milk comes to the boil again.
- Lower the heat and continue stirring until thick and creamy – about 10 minutes.
- Remove from the heat and allow to cool slightly.
- Separate the egg, mix the yolk and sugar, and stir into the semolina.
- Whisk the egg white until stiff and fold into the semolina.
- Rinse the mould with cold water, pour in the pudding.
- Cover and leave to set.

- *To make the sauce:* mix the juice and sugar, add the cinnamon stick and bring to the boil.
- Mix the potato starch with the water.
- Add to the juice and stir until it comes to the boil again.
- Lower the heat and cook gently for a further 2 minutes or until thickened.
- Cover and cool.

PRESENTATION

- Turn the pudding onto a serving platter.
- Remove the cinnamon stick from the sauce and pour some of it over the top of the pudding. Serve the remaining sauce separately.

Trommelkoek – Steamed Fruit Pudding

INGREDIENTS *for a 1.5 lt (3 pt; 6 cup) pudding basin*
For the pudding
  75 g (2 ½ oz; ½ cup) **currants**
  75 g (2 ½ oz; ½ cup) **raisins**
  15 g (½ oz) **baker's yeast or 1 tsp. dried yeast**
  350 ml (¾ pt; 1 ½ cups) **milk**
  250 g (8 oz; 1 ⅔ cups) **flour**
  ½ tsp. salt
  1 egg
  50 g (2 oz; ⅓ cup) + 1 tbsp. **butter**
  2 tbsp. sugar
  1 tbsp. grated lemon zest
  25 g (1 oz; ¼ cup) **ground almonds**

For the sauce
  50 g (2 oz; ⅓ cup) **butter**
  100 g (3 oz; ½ cup) **Dutch stroop, or syrup**

PREPARATION
- Wash and dry the currants and raisins.
- Dissolve the yeast in the milk.
- Sieve the flour and salt into a bowl, beat in the dissolved yeast.
- Lightly beat the egg, melt 50 g (2 oz; ⅓ cup) butter and beat both into the flour to make a smooth batter.
- Stir in the prepared fruit, lemon zest and sugar.
- Grease the pudding basin with the remaining butter and sprinkle with the almonds.
- Pour the batter into the prepared basin and let it rise for 30 minutes.
- Cover the basin, using greaseproof paper and string.
- Put into a large pan, pour in enough water to come to about 2.5 cm (1 inch) below the rim of the basin.
- Bring to the boil, cover the pan and simmer the pudding for 1 ½ hours, adding more boiling water if necessary.

- *To make the sauce:* melt the butter, add the syrup and heat through but do not boil.

PRESENTATION

- Turn the pudding onto a platter. Serve with the warm sauce.

Sugar – a Dutch success story

In former times, all sugar was produced from tropical cane which was transported across the seas to the sugar refineries of Europe; Amsterdam was the world leader in this field in the Golden Age of the 17th century.

Sugar was then an essential element in the chemists' preparations but as far as the general public went it was definitely the preserve of the rich; three gold pieces would just about buy a kilo of the cheapest variety. So expensive was it that to use it as a drink sweetener, the sugar, which was produced as a hard cone, used to be suspended over the table so that you could raise your cup of tea or coffee until the point of the cone just touched the liquid.

The sugar revolution came in the time of Napoleon when it was discovered that sugar of the same quality as that from cane could be extracted from beet. This plant grew well in the damp, cold northern European climate, and very soon it replaced cane for the expanding local market; sugar became an affordable basic for all households.

There is a unique Dutch sugar called *basterdsuiker* (as a native English speaker I had some difficulty with this word... in truth I still do, thinking that the word had only one connotation...); a kinder explanation of the meaning would be 'residual' or 'leftover' sugar.

This is how it happened: to produce clear white refined sugar the moulded sugar breads, as these sugar cones were called, had to be cleared of as much of the moist syrup as possible; water was allowed to drip on the moulds very slowly, washing the syrup through. In its turn this residue crystalised as it dried and as a cheap by-product it was bought by the ever penny-conscious bakers. To their surprise, those 18th century bakers found that it dissolved more evenly in their breads and biscuits than the pure refined sugar and indeed this *basterd* has been the Dutch baker's dream sugar ever since. There are many people in The Netherlands who have childhood memories of what was once a very special treat – slices of fresh white bread, spread with butter and sprinkled with moist brown sugar.

Basterd is a fine, almost powdered sugar and it comes in three colours, each with its slightly different taste, the darker ones containing more syrup. It is important to store this kind of sugar in a cool dry place or you may end up with a big hard lump of *basterd*...

Here are some of its uses:
the white – for ice creams, desserts, sauces, biscuits;
the brown – for brewing and the baking of pancakes, dark breads and biscuits, also delicious sprinkled on yoghurt;
and the light brown or yellow – also for breads and biscuits.
Wherever a recipe in this book asks for castor sugar you can use one of the *basterds*.

And finally another Dutch sugar speciality, also made from sugar beet – *stroop*; this is a dark aromatic sugar syrup, less refined and with a stronger flavour than golden syrup, much thicker than maple syrup. *Stroop*, dribbled over every pancake, sweet or savoury, is a 'must', and it is an important ingredient in the steamed pudding.

Tulips from Amsterdam

Flowers – a way of life for the people of The Netherlands

The skies may be grey, the landscape and horizons indistinguishable in the damp cheerless mist, but step inside any Dutch home and you are transported into a lush jungle of verdant foliage and varicoloured floral arrangements. The window sills of homes and offices alike are crowded with a wall of plants whose profusion seems to shout defiance at the perennial gloom without. Walk any residential way at night and glimpse the glow of family living almost hidden behind the greenery; there are few woven curtains pulled against the prying world – 'we have nothing to hide,' the houses seem to say, 'look in (if you can!), all is neat and above board.'

For the Dutch more than any other nation, with the exception perhaps of the Japanese, plants and flowers are an important part of living. Neatly laid flower gardens surround the suburban houses, and in the cities balconies and window ledges are alive with growing. No market day is complete without one or more stalls displaying plants for in-and-out-of-doors and the cut flower vendors do a brisk trade in hail or shine. Nor do you have to wait for market day, as there seems to be a flower shop or kiosk on every other corner, even on the garage forecourt the bouquets vie with petrol for a place.

Lesson number one for the newcomer to this country is flower etiquette. Nobody arrives for dinner without offering their hosts a bunch of blooms, always ten or more – less might be considered a gaffe. A new neighbour in the street?... the 'welcome' potted plants are in the door before the removal man has started on his task; and have you ever been run over by a commuter cyclist balancing umbrella, briefcase and a birthday bouquet against a howling gale? Whether it is a birth, wedding, or anniversary, your friend or colleague will expect a floral tribute. And maybe there is no reason at all when a spouse offers flowers with an-end-of-workday kiss.

No, you do not need to take a course in floral arranging, just mention the word *kado* (adapted from the French for a present), and if not already packaged, so your choice of colour, kind and cost will be skilfully assembled, wrapped in crinkly cellophane and finished off with spiralled ribbons. It is a joy just standing among the tantalizing array of possibilities, a delight which never palls.

It is no surprise then, that the unofficial national symbol of this country is a flower – the tulip. The history of the tulip in The Netherlands is one of enterprise and speculation, scientific endeavour and fanatic fascination. Here in the tulip story is truly an example of the Dutch paradox: how is it that a simple, scentless flower, which blooms for but a few short weeks, is highly susceptible to disease and so might not bloom at all, could yet become a priceless treasure, a prize of such speculative value that not so long ago, men were prepared to mortgage their all? It is a tale of how the levelheaded Dutch literally took leave of their senses.

The cult of the tulip is well documented. The flower was already extremely popular in medieval Turkey where the tulip featured prominently in the formal gardens, not in massed array but spaced carefully so that each precious bloom could stand alone to be fully admired by all. The period was called the Tulip Age and there were lavish festivals during the tulip season. The artists of the Ottoman Empire drew and painted the blooms on every kind of tile and pottery piece; it was often the Needle Tulip with its thin pointed petals which they depicted. This species is coming back into its own after years in the 'unfashionable' wilderness.

And so it was that an ambassador to the Ottoman court dispatched some bulbs to his native home in Vienna; the year was 1554. He is responsible for the name too, for he misunderstood the comparison being drawn by his Turkish hosts as they likened, not the flower but the petal shape of their *lalé* bloom to a… here it was that the ambassador got very confused, was it *dulband* they said, which in Dutch is *tulband*, a turban? Whatever the explanation, turbans they have been ever since!

It was in Vienna during this same period, that the famous botanist Carolius Clusius first saw the tulips. Not long after, in the newly laid botanical garden in the university city of Leiden, where he had just become Professor of Botany, Clusius began to cultivate and then experiment with the exotic bulbs. Once the secrets of the bulb were his he would sell selected ones; he anticipated great sales. That was his plan, but poor Clusius, he was no business man, for little did he realize that by so jealously guarding his tulips he fanned an obsession in other horticulturists. And so it happened that one night, creeping into the gardens under cover of darkness, robbers stole all his precious plants; the tulip was released onto a receptive open market.

For the next hundred years the popularity of this spring flower grew and grew. The gardeners cultivated, the chemists experimented, and the wealthy paid increasingly high prices; the tulip had become quite a status symbol. Where today's café habitués might argue over the sporting results or pontificate about the political trends, in 17th century Amsterdam the talk was all about the latest, newest, perhaps as yet unseen, variation on the tulip scene. If you overheard whispers of '...a Chimney Sweeper and a Painted Lady in the same bed...' or that 'the Bride of Enkhuizen was just a bit passé,' would you not be excited?

By 1634 The Netherlands was in the grip of tulipomania. At first everyone seemed to win, as rich and poor alike were caught up in the craze; by the end of 1636 there were single bulbs on offer for as much as 5000 florins. A workman might offer his livelihood tools, a nobleman his mansion and lands, all for a bulb as yet unproven. Tulips were the stakes in the world's first speculation bubble and like all such frenzies, in the spring of 1637, the bubble burst. It was no wonder that there were even some who suffered from tulipophobia and could not pass a bloom without lashing out at it with whatever came to hand.

But the moment of madness passed; though the value of the tulip as a commercial prospect did not. Today there are some 16,000 hectares of land given over to the annual cultivation of eight billion bulbs, most are destined for the export market. And for the locals and visitors alike there are a further six million on show every year in the grounds of the *Keukenhof* mansion. Nowhere is spring more compactly displayed than in these famous gardens, set in the heart of the bulb district of South Holland. The whole kaleidoscope of spring blooms are on show in pretty garden settings and they provide the perfect contrast to the dramatic ribbons of colour in the profitable bulb fields which surround them.

Spring is indisputably The Dutch season, cultivation an integral part of The Dutch way of life.

A Spring Dinner

Spring at last as we go shopping for this seasonal dinner; put aside the monotony of winter and rejoice in the first bunches of spring offerings. Sad would be the day if we were completely to lose sight of seasonal differences; nothing compares with the flavour of the first of the year's crop.

Voorjaarsgroentesoep met Balletjes
Spring Vegetable Soup with Tiny Meatballs

Saffraanbrood – Saffron Bread

~

Gekruid Lamsvlees uit de Oven – Herbed Roast Lamb

Knoflook-aardappelpuree – Garlic Potato Purée

Roergebakken Wilde Spinazie – Stir-fried Wild Spinach

~

Rabarbercompote – Compote of Rhubarb

Kwarkmousse met Limoen – Lime Quark Mousse

Amandelkoekjes – Almond Biscuits

Voorjaarsgroentesoep met Balletjes
Spring Vegetable Soup with Tiny Meatballs

The choice of vegetables for this spring soup is very much a matter of what is available, the only criterion should be to seek out a contrast of colours and textures. Meatballs feature in many Dutch soups, in this recipe they are really tiny ones; they could also be made from minced chicken or beef. If you are too short of time to make your own stock you may be able to find the readymade jars of *fond;* this clear unsalted stock is concentrated so it can be diluted one to one with water.

Vermicelli was one of the first pastas to be used in the Dutch kitchen. It can be found in three sizes, the best for this soup is the finest, (called 'angel's hair' by some and 'little worms' by others – take your pick!), just take a handful and crumble it into the soup at the last minute; the pasta strands should not be much longer than the chopped vegetables.

INGREDIENTS

500 g (1 lb; 2 cups) **mixed spring vegetables** (cauliflower, baby carrots, leeks, celery, mangetout, courgette – any combination)
250 g (½ lb) **minced veal**
1 tsp. **tomato purée**
a pinch of nutmeg
1 tbsp. **cream**
1 lt (2 pts; 1 qt) **stock**
50 g (2 oz) **vermicelli**
salt and freshly ground black pepper

PREPARATION

- Wash and prepare the vegetables, cut into small pieces.
- Mix the minced veal with the tomato purée, nutmeg and cream. Season to taste with salt and pepper and roll into marble-sized balls.
- Cook the meatballs in a little water for 2 minutes, drain and set aside.

- Bring the stock to the boil, add the prepared vegetables and cook for about 10 minutes or until just tender.
- Add the meatballs.
- Just before serving, crumble the vermicelli into the soup and cook for a further minute.
- Season with salt and pepper and serve.

Saffraanbrood – Saffron Bread

In the saffron plaited loaf Anneke uses *kwark* – quark, for a light and easily digested loaf; as available in The Netherlands quark is a fresh, low fat, smooth curd cheese; if unobtainable use any smooth curd cheese. The traditional plaited breads which are made with butter and eggs are very rich; here quark makes a healthy substitute as well as being a good source of protein. Quark is very versatile and is used in two of this month's recipes: the saffron bread and the lime mousse. On other occasions you could mix it with a little milk or cream to give a smoother consistency before simply spreading it on bread with a blob of jam or using it in place of cream with fresh fruit. When it comes to plaiting the loaf, work with three strands; I gather that those more experienced than myself can weave four, even six strands of dough. Brushing the dough with a little cream before baking gives a lighter golden finish to the loaf than an egg wash.

100 ml (3 fl oz; scant ½ cup) milk
⅛ tsp. saffron threads
15 g (½ oz) baker's yeast or 1 tsp. dried yeast
1 tbsp. sugar
250 g (½ lb; 1 ⅔ cups) plain flour
½ tsp. salt
50 g (2 oz; ¼ cup) quark
25 g (1 oz; 2 tbsp.) butter
1 tsp. grated orange zest
a little cream

PREPARATION

- Warm the milk.
- Infuse the saffron in the milk for 10 minutes.
- Dissolve the yeast and sugar in the saffron milk.
- Sieve the flour and salt into a bowl, make a well in the middle, add the dissolved yeast mixture and work into a third of the flour.
- Add the quark, butter and orange zest.
- Knead into a smooth and elastic ball.
- Cover the dough and leave until it has doubled in volume.
- Punch the air out of the dough and divide into three equal parts. Form each into a 20 cm (8 inch) long tapering strand.
- Press the three ends together, plait the strands and tuck the ends under.
- Transfer to a baking sheet; cover and leave to prove until it has again doubled in volume.
- Preheat the oven to 200°C/390°F.
- Brush the loaf with a little cream .
- Bake the loaf for 30 minutes, reduce heat to 175°C/350°F and bake for a further 10 minutes.
- Cool on a wire rack.

Gekruid Lamsvlees uit de Oven – Herbed Roast Lamb

I have been in The Netherlands for close on ten years and it is only recently that lamb is available at the regular meat counter. Looking through any traditional Dutch cook book one is hard pressed to find any recipes for lamb, and one never finds a mutton recipe. To date the reason for this omission remains a mystery and most (over 80%) of Dutch lamb continues to be exported. There is a slow improvement in the amount of lamb sold generally, though it is much more likely to appear on a restaurant menu than at the family table. The local Texel lamb is excellent; this breed has been carefully cross-bred from the hardy island species and they are raised throughout the country. The home product is much prized by connoisseurs from late spring until the end of October.

INGREDIENTS

1 kg (2 lbs) **boned leg of lamb** (plus the bone)

For the stuffing
2 cloves garlic
50 g (2 oz) **smoked bacon**
1 tsp. **rosemary**
1 tsp. **thyme**
1 tsp. **grainy mustard**
salt and freshly ground pepper
50 g (2 oz; 3 tbsp.) **butter**
125 g (4 oz; 1 cup) **onion**
125 g (4 oz; ½ cup) **carrot**
125 g (4 oz; ½ cup) **celery**
1 **bay leaf**
250 ml (½ pt; 1 cup) **fruity red wine**
1 tbsp. **red wine vinegar**
1 tsp. **tomato purée**

PREPARATION

- Preheat the oven to 175°C / 350°F.
- Peel and chop the garlic with the bacon, rosemary and thyme; mix

with the mustard, salt and pepper.
- Cut a pocket into the lamb and stuff with this mixture. Season the meat with salt and pepper and rub with the butter.
- Peel the onion and carrot and trim the celery; chop all the vegetables and put into a roasting pan with the bay leaf and the bone.
- Place the meat on top of the vegetables and roast for 20 minutes. Lower the heat to 150°C/300°F and roast for a further 50 minutes.
- Remove the meat from the pan, wrap in foil and keep warm.
- Remove the bone and the bay leaf.
- Purée the vegetables and the cooking liquid and transfer to a small pan; add the wine, vinegar and tomato purée, season to taste with salt and pepper.
- Bring to the boil and simmer for a few minutes.

PRESENTATION
- Slice the lamb and serve each slice with a little sauce. Pass the remainder of the sauce separately.

Knoflook-Aardappelpuree – Garlic Potato Purée

This purée combines very well with the lamb, but did you take fright as I did when first reading the recipe? A whole head of garlic? Be assured that by roasting the whole bulb, which you can do while the lamb is roasting, you get a delicious nutty flavour; your friends will be still talking to you after dinner and you will not even have to pass the anecdotal parsley! The purée could be made some time in advance and then put into the oven for 20 minutes or so before serving to give it a crispy golden topping.

Lovage, or sea parsley, has a strong celery flavour and is particularly good with mashed root vegetables and potatoes. It is usually the first herb to make its appearance in the spring herb garden; if the fresh leaves are not available use the seeds instead to give a real lift to all your purées and soups.

INGREDIENTS

1 whole head of garlic
1 tbsp. oil
1 kg (2 lb) floury potatoes
125 ml (¼ pt; ½ cup) cream or milk
25 g (1 oz; 2 tbsp.) butter
salt and freshly ground black pepper
a few sprigs of lovage

PREPARATION

- Preheat oven to 175°C/350°F.
- Slice the top off the unpeeled head of garlic, rub with the oil and put into a small ovenproof dish and bake for about 30 minutes or until very soft.
- Peel and cut the potatoes, put in a pan with just enough water to cover; bring to the boil.
- Lower the heat, cover and cook for about 20 minutes or until tender.
- Mash the potatoes with any remaining cooking liquid, squeeze the softened garlic out of the skins onto the potatoes and mix in.
- Add the cream and butter.
- Season to taste with salt and pepper.
- Chop the lovage leaves and fold into the purée.

Roergebakken Wilde Spinazie – Stir-fried Wild Spinach

Wild spinach or spinach beet has a coarser leaf and stem and a more pronounced flavour than the common variety, it is also somewhat easier to wash. The plumped currants give an extra lift to this simple vegetable and the whole dish can be prepared in minutes.

INGREDIENTS

1 tbsp. currants
1 ½ kg (3 lbs) wild spinach
2 spring onions
2 tbsp. oil
salt and freshly ground black pepper

PREPARATION

- Soak the currants in water to cover.
- Trim the stalks and wash the spinach thoroughly in plenty of water, drain.
- In a large pan cook the spinach for about 5 minutes without adding any water, turning it over as necessary. Drain and cut.
- Slice the spring onions and gently fry in the oil until soft.
- Drain the currants.
- Add the spinach and currants to the onions and toss until heated through.
- Season to taste with salt and pepper.

Rabarber Compote – Compote of Rhubarb

One of the first harbingers of spring is the early rhubarb, and it is undoubtedly the best time to enjoy it as the flavour is deliciously subtle; the stalks are still quite thin and pale, the leaves almost yellow. It is best to cook the rhubarb in a wide-bottomed pan with a lid, which can hold all the fruit in one layer. If you do not have this type of pan, use a frying pan and cover it with foil. Note that half the cooking time takes place off the heat, in this way the tender stalks will keep their shape and will not fall apart into stringy threads.

INGREDIENTS

750 g (1½ lb; 3 cups) **rhubarb**
125 ml (¼ pt; ½ cup) **water**
100 g (3 oz; ½ cup) **sugar**
125 ml (¼ pt; ½ cup) **red port**

PREPARATION

- Trim and cut the rhubarb into 5 cm/ 2 inch pieces and set aside.
- Put the water into a pan, add the sugar and bring to the boil, stirring until the sugar is dissolved; add the port.
- Lay the prepared rhubarb in the syrup. Bring to the boil then simmer over a low heat for 2 minutes.
- Remove from the heat. Cover the pan and leave the rhubarb to finish cooking in the hot syrup.
- Spoon the cooled rhubarb carefully into a serving bowl with the syrup.

Kwarkmousse met Limoen – Lime Quark Mousse

INGREDIENTS

1 tsp. **gelatine**
2 **egg yolks**
1 tsp. **grated lime zest**
1 tbsp. **lime juice**
100 g (3 oz; ½ cup) **sugar**
250 g (½ lb; 1⅓ cups) **quark**
125 ml (¼ pt; ½ cup) **cream**

PREPARATION

- In a small pan sprinkle the gelatine over a tablespoon of water, leave for one minute, then dissolve over a gentle heat.
- Beat the egg yolks with the lime zest, juice and the sugar until pale and thick.
- Beat the quark and dissolved gelatine into the egg mixture.
- Whip the cream separately and fold into the egg mixture.
- Pour into a serving bowl, cover and chill until set.

Amandelkoekjes – Almond Biscuits

INGREDIENTS *for approximately 12 biscuits*

150 g (5 oz; 1 cup) **plain flour**
50 g (2 oz; ½ cup) **ground almonds**
40 g (1½ oz; 3 tbsp.) **castor sugar**
100 g (3 oz; 6 tbsp.) **butter**
1 **egg yolk**
2 tbsp. **water**

PREPARATION

- Sieve the flour into a bowl, add the almonds and sugar.
- Cut the cold butter into small pieces and rub into the flour until it resembles coarse breadcrumbs.
- Mix the egg yolk and water; add to the flour.
- Knead just long enough to form a soft dough.
- Cover the dough and leave to rest in a cool place for 30 minutes.
- Preheat the oven to 180°C/360°F.
- On a floured surface roll out the dough to a 3 mm (⅛ inch) thickness. Cut out the biscuits with a round fluted cutter and place on an ungreased baking sheet.
- Gather the scraps, roll out and repeat.
- Bake for 15 minutes or until the biscuits are lightly browned.
- Cool on a wire rack.

Let's Celebrate

Birthdays and anniversaries; ever prominent on the Dutch social calendar

It has been said that the Dutch are a serious race, due in part, the argument goes, to their harsh environment and strict beliefs. But for anyone who has lived in this country, for even a short time, this turns out to be very far from the whole story. The people of The Netherlands love to celebrate, any excuse is enough for a party. Climate and dogmas are cast aside as young and old enter into the spirit of the event with an energy and creativity which amazes and astounds the outsider, as much for the ingenuity of the arrangements as for the vivacity of the participants.

Birthdays top the list of celebrations and no matter what your age there are certain rituals to be followed for these annual festivities. Every household, schoolroom or student flat has that essential list, the Birthday Calendar, usually found hanging in a well used place. It is indeed a serious social blunder to forget the anniversary of any family member, old school friend or office colleague.

But first the birth itself, within days of the arrival of a baby a notice of the glad tidings goes out to all the relatives and friends. When you call on mother and her babe with your small gift you are sure to be offered a *beschuit met muisjes*, a buttered rusk sprinkled with special pink and white sugared anise seeds. The origins of the little *muisjes* – mice, can only be guessed at, but they probably symbolize fertility. For years they were always pink and white though the manufacturers do now recognize that baby boys prefer blue. An old fashioned toast to the newborn was often made with a glass of *kandeel* – hot sweet wine blended with lemon juice, egg yolks and spices.

'The Birthday' is a special day – all day. Streamers, balloons and banners festoon the birthday person's house, inside and out, and small gifts are presented. Congratulations are exchanged, not just with the honoured one, but with each member of his or her family too; (it takes some getting used to, this delightful custom of being complimented on the birth of a father or husband – for I know I had no part in those events!). But it is not all about receiving, the birthday child takes goodies to school for the whole class; on his or her birthday, the employee offers cake to each member of the department; and the housewife... well, she holds Open House all day for her family and friends who drop by for morning coffee, afternoon tea or for a postprandial drink.

'Come at eight' or 'Come for *koffie met gebak*' – coffee with cake; this is an invitation which is not reserved just for birthdays and is a favourite way of entertaining in The Netherlands. Guests are invited after the family's early evening dinner; they will be offered coffee, or tea for the insomniacs, and a slice of cake; on a birthday evening it will be a special cream cake. Then after a second round of the coffee pot, cups and plates are cleared away and drinks and savouries are served. How many unsuspecting newcomers to this country have arrived at their hosts door promptly at eight thinking they were coming to dinner!

So important is the celebration of birthdays that the Dutch queen grants a Public Holiday for hers – 30th April, *Koninginnedag* – Queen's Day. This is in fact her mother Queen Juliana's birthday, but Queen Beatrix was born in January and it is not such party weather then. On the last day of April the whole nation is bedecked with royal House of Orange flags and bunting, and a free market day is allowed. Anyone can set up a stall, just chalk out your patch the night before, and then from dawn onwards you are permitted to sell your attic treasures and homemade wares, or just to entertain the crowd. The people of Amsterdam in particular, host a daylong street party which spreads over the whole city; no traffic moves as crowds throng the public ways. Afloat along the canals, broadside to broadside, are craft of every size and shape filled to the gunwales with party groups. Orange hats and faces abound, bakers windows turn every confection bright orange, flower stalls are stacked high with blooms grown orange for the day, music and laughter is everywhere and the toast of the town is *oranje bitter* – another variety of geneva, this one coloured… yes you have guessed – bright orange… an acquired taste!

One adult birthday is even more special – the 50th. It is said that fifty years into life man has reached the very peak of his powers of intellect and judgement and so he is entitled to become an *Abraham*. This tradition has its origins in the New Testament when, in amazement… 'they asked of Jesus: You are not yet fifty years old and You Have Seen Abraham?' For centuries the Dutch have celebrated this birthday with much festivity; there are huge quantities of streamers in honour of the birthday man, there may be a stuffed dummy in his likeness, dressed in his clothes and sitting in his favourite chair; that office round of cakes will have to be more special than usual. In return, a special Abraham cake will be offered – this is a giant flat biscuit in the shape of the prophet, maybe elaborately decorated, complete with golden crown and white beard and sometimes filled with a rich almond paste. Oh, and without doubt accompanied by a telling verse or two.

The fairer sex will be glad to hear that eventually Dutch ladies of that certain age were also recognized as reaching the pinnacle of wisdom and they now celebrate their *Sara* day with much the same fun and excitement.

Anniversaries too come in for special treatment, the 25th, 50th, 60th are well known, but there is a surprising Dutch observation – the 12 ½ or copper anniversary – half way to twenty five but hard to find the logic! Just another reason for a party, whether it is to fête years of a marriage, a partnership, business venture or whatever – 'let's celebrate'; Queen Beatrix for example, recently commemorated her 12 ½ years on the throne. No matter where you live or journey to in The Netherlands, sooner or later you will be joining in the ceremonial song:
Lang zal hij leven, lang zal hij leven in de gloria, in de gloria…
and at that point you raise your glass in the air with a loud
Hiep.. hiep.. hiep.. hoera, hiep.. hiep.. hiep.. hoera…

A Birthday Party

Entertaining friends and family in The Netherlands is often a coffee time affair and so this month's recipes concentrate on cakes and biscuits, not forgetting some savouries to go with drinks.

Appeltaart – Dutch Apple Tart

Boterkoek – Butter Tart

Slagroomtaart – Cream Cake

Jan Hagel – Almond and Cinnamon Biscuits

Weesper Moppen – Almond Rounds

Friese Dumkes – Spicy Finger Biscuits

Gevulde Komkommer en Kerstomaatjes
Stuffed Cucumber Cups and Cherry Tomatoes

Roze Pepervlinders – Pink Pepper Butterflies

Kaasbrood Borrelhapjes – Cheese Bread Canapés

Appeltaart – Dutch Apple Tart

This is made with a thick shortcrust pastry base, layers of sliced apple and dried fruits and a lattice of pastry on the top. Other fruits can be substituted. Sprinkle the dough with gelatine before adding the apples as this absorbs the apple juice and prevents the base from becoming too moist.

INGREDIENTS *for a 24 cm (10 inch) round tin*
    150 g (5 oz; 1 cup) **raisins and currants**
    3 tbsp. **rum**

For the pastry
    300 g (10 oz; 2 cups) **plain flour**
    200 g (7 oz; ¾ cup) **softened butter**
    100 g (3 oz; ½ cup) **sugar**
    1 **egg yolk**
    1 tsp. **grated lemon zest**

For the filling
    1 kg (2 lbs) **apples** (e.g. Elstar)
    1 tbsp. **lemon juice**
    2 tbsp. **sugar**
    1 tsp. **cinnamon**
    1 ½ tsp. **gelatine**
    50 g (2 oz; ¼ cup) **butter**

For serving
    125 ml (¼ pt; ½ cup) **cream**
    1 tbsp. **castor sugar**

- Wash and dry the fruit; add the rum and set aside.
- *To make the pastry:* Sift the flour into a bowl, mix in the butter, sugar, egg yolk and lemon zest. Continue mixing until a soft dough has formed.
- Cover and chill for about 30 minutes.

- Preheat the oven to 175°C/350°F.
- Grease the tin.
- Peel and core the apples, slice thinly and sprinkle with the juice.
- Mix together the sugar and cinnamon.
- Take three-quarters of the dough and press into the base and sides of the tin, sprinkle the base with the gelatine.
- Alternate layers of apple slices and dried fruit, sprinkle each with a little sugar/cinnamon, end with a layer of apple.
- Dot with the butter.
- Roll out the remaining dough into a rectangle.
- Cut into 1 cm (½ inch) wide strips and form a lattice over the fruit, sealing the ends. Brush with a little cream.
- Bake in the middle of the oven for 45 minutes, or until golden.
- Cool.
- Whip the cream with the castor sugar.

PRESENTATION

- Serve with whipped cream.
- A little cinnamon could be mixed into the cream.

Boterkoek – Butter Tart

Boterkoek is a thin, very buttery cake, a cross between shortbread and cake and it is served cut into small bite-sized pieces.

INGREDIENTS *for a 22 cm (9 inch) sandwich tin*

250 g (½ lb; 1⅔ cups) **plain flour**
a pinch of salt
200 g (7 oz; ¾ cup) **butter**

225 g (7 ½ oz; 1 ⅛ cups) **castor sugar**
a little milk

PREPARATION
- Preheat the oven to 225°C/440°F.
- Sieve the flour and salt into a bowl. Cut the cold butter into the flour using two knives.
- Add the sugar and knead quickly into a dough.
- Press evenly into the base of the tin.
- Using the back of a fork, make diagonal lines across the dough.
- Brush the surface with a little milk.
- Bake for 15-20 minutes or until golden brown on top, and the inside still moist.
- Cool in the tin then cut into small wedges.

Banketbakkerijen – cake shops

The cake shops in The Netherlands are a delight, such a tantalizing choice, pastries topped with fruits and exotic whirls of cream; rich chocolate and coffee cream slices, almond and hazelnut cakes and biscuits; it is very hard to resist. Truly this is a country where many people have a liking for the sweet things in life, in fact the Dutch lead the world stakes on consumption of sweets and cakes!

A very simple classic Dutch cake is often served at coffee time and is known simply as *cake*; it is like an English pound cake. *Cake* is served plain; not iced or sandwiched with jam.

Slagroomtaart – Cream Cake

For a birthday something more special than *cake* is called for and the hostess will probably order a *slagroomtaart*, but for those feeling adventurous, or who are far from a Dutch patisserie, Anneke includes her recipe here. It is best to make the sponge the day before and assemble the cake an hour or so before the guests arrive. The sponge base is cut into layers and sandwiched with cream and fruit, covered with thick cream and decorated with chocolates, the sides with nuts. The *umer* adds a lighter touch to the filling though you could use all cream, or a mixture of cream and yoghurt (See page 84).

INGREDIENTS *for a 26 cm (11 inch) springform tin*
>   100 g (3 oz; ⅔ cup) plain flour
>   100 g (3 oz; ⅔ cup) cornflour
>   a pinch of salt
>   6 eggs
>   100 g (3 oz; 1 cup) ground almonds
>   150 g (5 oz; ¾ cup) castor sugar
>   1 tsp. grated lemon zest
>   1 tbsp. brandy
>   2 tbsp. water

For the filling
>   1 tin/can mandarin oranges (312 g; 10 oz)
>   250 ml (1/2 pt; 1 cup) cream
>   250 g (½ pt; 1 cup) *umer*
>   50 g (2 oz; ¼ cup) castor sugar
>   1½ tsp. gelatine

To decorate
>   50 g (2 oz; ½ cup) flaked almonds
>   125 ml (¼ pt; ½ cup) cream
>   1 tbsp. icing sugar
>   ½ tsp. gelatine
>   100 g (3 oz) wafer chocolates

- *To make the cake:* Grease and flour the tin.
- Preheat the oven to 175°C/350°F.
- Sieve the flour, cornflour and salt.
- Separate the eggs.
- Beat the yolks with the ground almonds, half the sugar, lemon zest, brandy and water until thick and pale.
- Whisk the whites until frothy, then gradually add the remaining sugar and continue beating until very stiff.
- Gently fold a third of the sieved flour into the yolk mixture, then a third of the egg whites, continue alternating until all is incorporated.
- Transfer to the prepared tin and bake for 45 minutes.
- Remove the cake from the oven and leave in the tin for 10 minutes before turning out onto a wire rack.
- Cool for at least 3 hours or overnight.
- Rinse the tin for assembling the cake later.

- *To make the filling:* Drain the mandarin syrup into a bowl. Put 3 tablespoonfuls of this syrup into a small saucepan, sprinkle the gelatine over it, leave for 1 minute, then dissolve over a gentle heat. Remove from the heat and stir into the reserved syrup.
- Beat the cream and sugar adding the dissolved gelatine syrup gradually, continue beating until stiff.
- Set 14 mandarin segments aside, fold the remainder with the *umer* into the cream.

- *To assemble the cake:* Cut the cake into 3 layers.
- Put one layer of cake back into the tin.
- Spread one half of the cream mixture onto this layer.
- Cover with the second layer, spread with the remaining cream mixture and place the third layer on top, pressing it down gently .
- Chill for at least 30 minutes or until set.

- *Decoration:* Toast the flaked almonds for the decoration (this could be done in the oven as it warms for baking the cake), when golden, remove and set aside.

- In a small pan sprinkle the gelatine over a tablespoon of water, leave for 1 minute, then dissolve over a low heat.
- Beat the remaining cream and the sugar adding the dissolved gelatine gradually; continue beating until stiff.
- Remove the cake carefully from the tin and put onto a wire rack.
- Smooth three quarters of the cream over the top and sides, press the toasted almonds gently onto the sides, then transfer to a serving platter.

PRESENTATION
- With the remaining cream pipe 14 rosettes on the top of the cake; decorate with the reserved mandarin and the chocolates.

Koekjes – biscuits

There are endless variations on the biscuit theme, every area of the country promoting its own specialities. One custom to note is that shortcrust biscuits are usually served with coffee, and the drier crisper kinds with tea. Here are the names of some of the tea biscuits which you might like to search for in the Dutch stores: *Knappertjes, Zaanse Kermis, Frou-frou* and the more universally known – Marie biscuits. We offer you the recipes of three of the coffee time varieties: the *Jan Hagel* are said to originate in Amersfoort, a city in the heart of the country which has origins dating back to the earliest times and which give its name to yet another biscuit – the *Amersfoortse Kei* – this last word *Kei* means boulder. This biscuit celebrates the winning of a wager four centuries ago – a nine thousand kilo boulder was actually brought, I hesitate to say carried, into the city, and it is still there for all to see. The almond *Weesper Moppen* were first so named after a town near Amsterdam and the aniseed flavoured *Dumkes* come from the province of Friesland.

One of the most popular biscuits is the *Stroopwafel* from Gouda. These wafer thin waffles are sandwiched with syrup and can be bought fresh off the waffle stall, in packets or in attractive blue and white tins which make an excellent gift for the traveller; the recipe however, remains a professional secret.

Jan Hagel – Almond and Cinnamon Biscuits

INGREDIENTS *for approximately 50 biscuits*

250 g (½ lb; 1⅔ cups) **plain flour**
¼ tsp. baking powder
1 tsp. cinnamom
120 g (4 oz; ⅔ cup) **castor sugar**
180 g (6 oz; ¾ cup) **butter**
100 g (3 oz; 1 cup) **flaked almonds**
50 g (2 oz; ¼ cup) **sugar**

PREPARATION

- Sieve the flour, baking powder and cinnamon into a bowl, add the sugar.
- Cut the butter into small pieces and rub into the sieved flour until it resembles coarse breadcrumbs.
- With cold hands quickly knead into a ball.
- Cover and leave in a cool place for 30 minutes.
- Preheat the oven to 175°C / 350°F.
- Grease and flour a 30 × 40 cm (12 × 16 inch) baking sheet. Roll and press the dough onto the baking sheet.
- Sprinkle the top with the almonds and sugar and press gently into the dough.
- Bake for 20 minutes or until golden.
- Remove from the oven and immediately cut into 4 × 6 cm (2 × 3 inch) shapes. If left to cool too much, the biscuits will become brittle and will break as you cut them.

Weesper Moppen – Almond Rounds

INGREDIENTS *for approximately 30 biscuits*
300 g (10 oz; 1½ cups) **sugar**
250 g (½ lb; 2½ cups) **ground almonds**
2 small eggs
1 tsp. grated lemon zest

PREPARATION
- Line a baking sheet with greaseproof paper.
- Reserve 2 tablespoons of the sugar and mix the remainder with the ground almonds, eggs and lemon zest until you have a smooth paste.
- Put the paste onto a piece of plastic wrap and roll up in the wrap into a 4 cm (1½ inch) cylinder. Chill for at least 1 hour or until firm enough to handle.
- Preheat the oven to 225°c /440°F
- Unwrap the cylinder and roll it in the reserved sugar.
- Cut into 30 rounds (regularly dipping the cutter into water).
- Put the biscuits onto the baking sheet. Bake for about 10 minutes or until golden.

Friese Dumkes - Spicy Finger Biscuits

INGREDIENTS *for approximately 60 biscuits*
- 100 g (3 oz; ⅔ cup) **shelled hazelnuts**
- 1 tbsp. **aniseed**
- 125 g (4 oz; ½ cup) **butter**
- 100 g (3 oz; ½ cup) **soft brown sugar**
- 1 **egg**
- 250 g (½ lb; 1⅔ cups) **plain flour**
- a pinch of salt
- 1 tsp. cinnamon
- 1 tsp. ground ginger

PREPARATION:
- Preheat the oven to 175°C/350°F.
- Grease and flour a baking sheet.
- Grind the hazelnuts and aniseed and set aside.
- Cream the butter and sugar, add the egg and mix well.
- Sift the flour, salt, cinnamon and ginger; add the hazelnuts and aniseed and mix into the creamed butter and sugar until a soft dough is formed; cover and chill for 30 minutes.
- On a floured surface, roll the dough into a rectangle 1 cm (⅓ inch) thick and approximately 20 × 30 cm (10 × 12 inches).
- Cut into 2 × 4 cm (1 × 2 inch) strips and transfer to the baking sheet.
- Bake for 25 minutes or until golden.
- Remove from the oven and separate with a knife while still warm; cool on a wire rack.

Gevulde Komkommer en Kerstomaatjes
Stuffed Cucumber Cups and Cherry Tomatoes

INGREDIENTS

For the filling
+ 1 shallot
+ a clove of garlic
+ 50 g (2 oz; ¼ cup) carrot
+ ½ red pepper
+ 50 g (2 oz; ¼ cup) celery
+ 1 tbsp. oil
+ 1 tbsp. red wine vinegar
+ ¼ tsp. cayenne pepper
+ salt and freshly ground black pepper
+ 100 g (4 oz) slice ham – in one piece

To serve
+ 1 cucumber (approximately 500 g; 1 lb)
+ 250 g (½ lb) cherry tomatoes
+ a few sprigs of parsley

PREPARATION

- *To make the filling:* Peel the shallot, garlic and carrot, remove seeds and membrane from the red pepper, trim the celery; finely chop all the vegetables.
- Heat the oil in a frying pan and gently fry the vegetables for about 10 minutes or until soft.
- Stir in the vinegar and cayenne; simmer uncovered for a further 5 minutes until most of the liquid has evaporated.
- Season with salt and pepper and leave to cool.
- Dice the ham, mix into the cooled vegetables.
- Cover and leave to marinade for at least 2 hours, or overnight.
- *To serve:* Peel the cucumber, cut into 3 cm (1 inch) slices; scoop out enough of the seeds to form a small container.
- Cut the tops off the tomatoes and set aside; scoop out the seeds.
- Put a spoonful of the filling into the prepared vegetables.
- Chop the parsley.

- Arrange the stuffed vegetables on a serving platter; garnish the cucumber with the parsley; replace the tops onto the tomatoes.

Roze Pepervlinders – Pink Pepper Butterflies

INGREDIENTS *for approximately 50 biscuits*
- 100 g (3 oz; 1 cup) **grated cheese** (mature Gouda)
- 25 g (1 oz; 2 tbsp.) **softened butter**
- 1 **egg white**
- 1 tsp. **dried pink peppercorns**
- **salt and freshly ground black pepper**
- 250 g (½ lb) **puff pastry (fresh or frozen)**

PREPARATION
- Mix the cheese with the butter, egg white and peppercorns. Season to taste with salt and pepper; cover and set aside.
- Cut the (defrosted) pastry in half; roll each half into a 15 × 30 cm (6 × 12 inch) rectangle .
- Divide the cheese mixture in half.
- Take half of the cheese, spread one third down each side of the pastry rectangle, leaving a 2.5 × 30 cm (1 × 12 inch) gap down the middle.
- Fold the edges of the pastry into this gap, leaving a little space between them. Spread the remaining cheese mixture over one half of the newly formed rectangle. Fold again. Press down gently.
- Repeat with the other rectangle of pastry.
- Cover and chill for 30 minutes.
- Preheat the oven to 200°C /390°F.
- With a sharp knife cut the folded pastry into 1.5 cm (½ inch) strips.
- Transfer the strips onto a baking sheet which has been sprinkled with a little water.
- Bake for 15-20 minutes or until golden.
- Cool on a wire rack.

Kaasbrood Borrelhapjes – Cheese Bread Canapés

Canapés can look even more attractive on rounds of bread, so instead of using a 1 kg (2 lb; 4 cup) loaf tin, Anneke often uses three well greased 750 ml (1½ pt/ 3 cup) syrup tins with the tops cut off (some soup tins are also suitable). She is careful to shape the dough into a cylinder smaller than the tin to allow the dough to rise. To bake the bread in these tins the oven rack has to be in its lowest position and the tins are placed on it standing up. To remove the bread from the tin, tap it gently and ease the loaf out.
You could substitute 150 g (5 oz) cream cheese plus 100 g (3 oz; ½ cup) yoghurt for the quark.

INGREDIENTS *for a 1 kg (2 lb; 4 cup) loaf tin*
  30 g (1 oz) **baker's yeast**
  150 ml (5 fl oz; ½ cup + 1 tbsp.) **milk**
  500 g (1 lb; 3 ⅔ cups) **plain flour**
  1 tsp. **salt**
  100 g (3 oz; 1 cup) **grated cheese** (mature Gouda)
  250 g (½ lb; 1¼ cups) **quark**
  25 g (1 oz; 1 tbsp.) **softened butter**

PREPARATION
  • Grease the loaf tin (or tins – see note above).
  • Dissolve the yeast in the milk.
  • Mix the flour, salt and grated cheese; make a well in the middle, pour in the yeast mixture and mix into a third of the flour.
  • Add the quark and butter; knead into a smooth and elastic ball.
  • Cover the dough and leave until it has doubled in volume.
  • Punch the air out of the dough and press into a rectangle; then roll up tightly, tucking in the ends.
  • Put into the greased tin and leave to prove for a further 30 minutes.
  • Preheat the oven to 200°C/390°F.
  • Bake for 30 minutes. Turn down the oven to 175°C/350°F.
  • Remove the loaf from the tin, and put it back into the oven for a further 20 minutes.
  • Cool on a wire rack.

Suggested canapé spreads:

When the bread has cooled completely cut into thin slices of whatever shape or size desired and serve with one of the following canapé toppings.

- Cover the slices of bread with cream cheese and top with a slice of smoked salmon (cut to fit).
  Garnish with half a slice of cucumber.
  Decorate with a tiny sprig of dill.

- Mix softened butter with a little lemon zest and juice.
  Spread lemon butter on the slices of bread and top with thinly sliced radishes and a little cress.

- Mix together grated apple, lemon juice, a few drops of walnut oil and chopped walnuts.
  Butter the bread, top each slice with a spoonful of the nut mixture.

- Purée a fillet of smoked trout with a little butter, cream, and 1 tsp. tomato purée.
  Spread onto the slices of bread.
  Decorate with a little sour cream mixed with trout eggs and a few drops of lime juice.

Hidden Gold

White asparagus – forever a spring favourite

Spring fever is still in the air and the trees wear their luminous green; the summer crops are fledgling now and the countryside is alive with growing; but wait, what are those bare fields? Not flat furrowed earth with emerging green shoots like the rest, but rather, neatly topped mounds which range in long fat rows throwing earthy shadows on the sandy soil – no signs of spring in evidence there. Worry not, these are no barren Dutch lands, but asparagus beds which grow their precious harvest under cover for fear of the ever greening rays of light.

Wild asparagus is said to have originated in Asia and come west through Greece and Italy. The Romans were enjoying it as early as 148 B.C.; there is a description of its cultivation in a book on farming methods written by Cato the Elder. Some 150 years later the great Emperor Augustus is said to have chived his slothful civil servants along by shouting at them 'Get that problem solved in… in… less time than it takes to cook… eh… asparagus.' One can't help but wonder if the chefs overcooked it in those days!

Seventeen centuries later Louis xiv 'discovered' cultivated asparagus for more northern climes and the monastery gardeners were encouraged to grow Argenteuil asparagus, as the white asparagus was named, for the tables of the aristocracy; and so popular was it among the Royal gourmets that the 17th century gardeners even heated the asparagus beds to prolong the season. This white asparagus is still much in demand in northern France, Germany, Belgium and The Netherlands, while other markets prefer the green shoots. In the last few years, for the first time, green asparagus has been found in the Dutch greengrocers', but it is usually the foreigners who buy it. As the saying goes in Dutch: *wat een boer niet kent, eet hij niet* – what a farmer does not know he does not eat! Old habits die hard.

Traditionally the local white asparagus season should not begin before
the Dutch queen's official birthday holiday on 30th April, but is more
likely to be 6th May – it depends on the severity of the winter, and the
warmth of the spring. The last shoots must be cut before the sun goes
down on the feast of St. Jan on 24th June. Imports and glasshouse
growing have lengthened the season, but for the connoisseurs it is just
not the real thing.

During these short seven weeks, the grower and his workers will move
up and down the asparagus beds in the first light of dawn and maybe
even a second time towards the end of the day. Basket on one arm,
cutter in the other hand, bent double as with x-ray eyes they cut out
the seemingly invisible shoots, smoothing back the earth again and
again with the flat base of their metal baskets.

It is probably the most labour intensive crop there is, but for some the
rewards justify the effort. And the plant itself is not unmindful of all
the care lavished on it as this story illustrates: early one morning an
asparagus cutter came to the end of the last row of embedded shoots,
and as he straightened his aching back, he realized that his wedding
ring must have slipped off, and was probably now buried in one of the
asparagus beds; gone for ever he thought sadly. Some three years later
he was easing a juicy spear out of the ground when *lo and behold,*
something glinted in the sunlight… his wedding band circling a white
finger of asparagus.

The difference between the green and the white asparagus is not one
of type, but of growing methods. The former has a stronger flavour, is
easier to harvest, quicker to cook and the plant is allowed to develop
naturally, shoots and foliage at the same time, all above ground. To
produce the 'white', young male hybrids are embedded in mounds of
earth built up to about 45 cm; then, the farmer must wait some two
years until the new spring sun can warm his hidden gold into growth.
Only after the harvest time are the green ferns allowed to grow
through the earth for their season above ground.

There are experiments being carried out with artificially high beds, which can support a lot more plants per square metre than in the fields and which are capable of being heated. While it would not be such a backbreaking a job for the pickers, it is doubtful whether the costs could be economical.

Asparagus is best suited to sandy soil, and it was in the dune lands of 's-Gravenzande and in Brabant that it was first grown commercially in The Netherlands; today the major asparagus region is in north Limburg. Here on the heathlands, which is poor soil for most crops, the asparagus' deep roots find an enriching milieu. And as was certainly a feature in the early production years, the largely Catholic farmers have had numerous family members to call on as pickers during the short harvest season (as with mushrooms).

From the late 1940's onwards there has been a big increase in production, not only in the sale of fresh spears, but also for the canneries. Though the fresh asparagus does not have a long shelf life, there is little doubt that it remains a sought after luxury item in the gourmet vegetable market.
On many menus worldwide asparagus is an accompaniment, garnish or first course delicacy; it makes an excellent salad, soup or quiche in any country, but in the 'white asparagus' regions of France and northern Europe, it is a main meal in itself and is traditionally served warm, with new potatoes, thin slices of cold ham and hardboiled eggs and lots of melted butter; or even nicer, a creamy hollandaise sauce. This sauce is said to have been created by French Huguenots exiled in Holland, hence its name.

Eating asparagus has its problems for the masters of etiquette: do you tuck your napkin round your neck and with fingers lift and dip the tender tips into the buttery sauce, suck out the succulent flesh, discard the stringy layer and call for a finger bowl? Do you try it with a combination of fingers and a helping fork to support the heavy spear? Or, as many Dutch do, eat it demurely with a knife and fork – but then this is a land where even a sandwich is eaten this way. For the asparagus question there doesn't seem to be a definitive answer.

An Asparagus Dinner

~

In many parts of The Netherlands there are asparagus festivals at this time of year and white asparagus in particular features prominently among the 'Dishes of the Day' in just about every restaurant, and in just about every section of the menu too – there is even a sweet asparagus ice cream.

In this May menu Anneke has made much use of both green and white asparagus.

Haringtartaar met een Bieslook Roomsaus
Herring Tartar with a Creamy Chive Sauce

Soep van Groene Asperges en Broccoli
Green Asparagus and Broccoli Soup

Maïsmeelbroodjes – Cornmeal Rolls

~

Witte Asperges, Kwarteleitjes en Gekookte Ham, Nieuwe Aardappeltjes
White Asparagus, Quail's Eggs and Boiled Ham, New Potatoes

~

Citroentaart met Aardbeien – Lemon Tart with Strawberries

Fresh from the sea – the Dutch herring

For those new to the Dutch culinary scene we would like to introduce you to one of the country's great uncooked specialities – the herring. The herring season begins with *vlaggetjesdag* – flag day. On the last Saturday of May, from the ports of Scheveningen and IJmuiden, with flags flying and bands playing, the fishing fleets set out to sea on a race to see who can return with the first of the new season's catch. The first cask of herring passed by the inspectors is delivered to Her Majesty the Queen and the season is officially declared 'open'.

The shoals of four year old herrings, then considered in their prime, will be massing somewhere in the North Sea to take part in their annual spawning migration. Once netted each fish is cleaned, lightly salted and on today's modern vessels, frozen for a minimum of 48 hours.

For the next two months every fish shop in the Netherlands will advertise the *Hollandse nieuwe* – or *maatjesharing* – this name comes from the Dutch word for maiden, *maagdje*. The quality of each season's new herring is discussed by every 'expert' as a matter of national importance, helped no doubt by a glass of geneva or two. With the advent of freezing techniques the season can last well into the year; formerly the later catches were preserved in a much higher concentration of salt and were called *zoute haring*, these had to be rinsed before they too were eaten raw.

It is fascinating to watch the fishmongers skin and bone the fish in a few deft movements, they leave the two fillets just attached to the tail for easy eating… that is the theory anyway. Having ordered your *nieuw*, finely chopped onions are offered, you heap one fillet with some of these, lift the fish by its tail and lower the piece into your mouth, all without dropping too much of the onion – definitely a challenge for the consumer.

Haringtartaar met een Bieslook Roomsaus
Herring Tartar with Creamy Chive Sauce

As May is a special month for this salty fish, Anneke begins the meal with an innovative herring tartar; the accompanying creamy sauce compliments the saltiness of the fish, the whole lifted by a touch of aniseed. In the absence of fresh herring, make a different tasting dish with smoked salmon or trout, the other ingredients and the method would remain the same.

INGREDIENTS *for 4 servings*
   4 filleted herring
   1 cucumber (approximately 500 g; 1 lb)
   2 large tomatoes
   ½ tart apple
   1 spring onion
   1 tsp. anise flavoured liqueur
   250 ml (½ pt; 1 cup) **unsalted fish stock**
   a small bunch of chives
   125 g (4 oz; ½ cup) *crème fraîche*
   salt and freshly ground black pepper

PREPARATION
- Remove the tail piece and any remaining bones from the filleted herring. Cut each fillet first into 4 long strips, then across into small pieces.
- Divide the cucumber in half, set one half aside for garnish. Peel and remove the seeds from the tomato, reserving one for garnish.
- Chop the cucumber, tomato and apple; thinly slice the spring onions
- Mix these ingredients with the herring and liqueur; season with salt and pepper.
- Cover and chill.

- *To make the sauce:* Boil the fish stock until there are 2 tablespoons left, remove from the heat and cool.

- Snip the chives and mix into the reduced stock with the *crème fraîche*.
- Season with salt and pepper. Cover and chill.

- Halve the reserved cucumber lengthways and scoop out the seeds, slice thinly; cut the tomato into 12 strips

PRESENTATION
- Mould the herring mixture onto 4 small plates, spoon the sauce round the fish and garnish with the cucumber and tomato.

Soep van Groene Asperges en Broccoli
Green Asparagus and Broccoli Soup

Germans call broccoli 'asparagus cabbage' and the two are a natural combination in this easy soup. Having cooked the tips and the broccoli florets, it is a good idea to rinse them immediately in cold water, then leave them to drain; in this way they keep their fresh green colour.

INGREDIENTS
500 g (1 lb) **green asparagus**
250 g (½ lb) **broccoli**
25 g (1 oz; 2 tbsp.) **butter**
50 g (2 oz; ¼ cup) **each of carrot, onion, celery**
50 g (2 oz) **bacon**
1 lt (2 pts; 1 qt) **chicken stock**
1 **egg yolk**
1 tsp. **cornflour**
100 ml (3 fl oz; scant ½ cup) **cream**
salt and freshly ground black pepper

PREPARATION
- Cut 5 cm (2 inch) long tips from the asparagus, trim and reserve the stalks; separate the broccoli heads into tiny florets, trim, peel

and reserve the stalks.
- Cook the tips and florets in a little water until just tender, but still crunchy. Drain and rinse in cold water. Set aside.
- Peel the carrot and onion, trim the celery; finely chop with the asparagus and broccoli stalks and the bacon.
- Put the chopped vegetables and bacon into a pan with the butter and gently fry for about 5 minutes or until soft.
- Add the stock, bring to the boil and simmer until the vegetables are tender; purée.
- Mix the egg yolk with the cornflour and cream and stir into the soup. Heat through but do not boil.
- Season with salt and pepper.

PRESENTATION
- Garnish with the cooked asparagus tips and broccoli florets.

Maïsmeelbroodjes – Cornmeal Rolls

There is a greater interest today in cooking with natural ingredients which have been obtained from as close to source as possible, a real return to the basics of yesteryear. As result, many old flour windmills are being brought back to life in The Netherlands; stone ground corn, rye and wholemeal flours are in demand. Using a coarse cornmeal gives these rolls a crunchy bite and with their pale yellow colour they just call for a generous spread of Dutch *boerenroomboter* – farm butter.

INGREDIENTS

15 g (½ oz) **baker's yeast or 1 tsp. dried yeast**
150 ml (5 fl oz; ½ cup + 2 tbsp.) **water**
200 g (7 oz; 1⅓ cups) **plain flour**
¼ tsp. salt
50 g (2 oz; ⅓ cup) **coarse cornmeal + 1 tbsp.**

PREPARATION

- Dissolve the yeast in the water.
- Sieve the flour and salt into a bowl. Mix in the 50 g (2 oz; ⅓ cup) cornmeal, make a well in the middle, pour in the dissolved yeast and with a fork mix into the flour mixture.
- Knead into a smooth and elastic ball.
- Cover the dough and leave until it has doubled in volume.
- Punch the air out of the dough and divide into 12 portions. Form each into a roll.
- Brush the rolls with a little water and sprinkle with the remaining cornmeal.
- Cover the rolls and prove for a further 10 minutes.
- Heat the oven to 225°C / 440°F.
- Transfer the rolls to a greased baking sheet and bake for 15 minutes.
- Cool on a wire rack.

Witte Asperges, Kwarteleitjes en Gekookte Ham
White Asparagus, Quail's Eggs and Boiled Ham

Buy the asparagus as fresh as you can and if it has to be kept for a day or so, wrap in a damp tea towel and store in a plastic bag in the refrigerator. When preparing the white asparagus you should peel the stems and cut off the woody ends. Green asparagus is even easier to prepare, you need only trim the ends. Most people prefer to steam their asparagus and there are special steamers on the market which are designed specifically to take the tall asparagus spears so that the ends are in water, while the upright tips cook in the steam. You could however, use an ordinary pan, but it must be big enough for the spears to be laid flat. If you do not have a special asparagus serving platter, which allows the water to drain into the base, then place the cooked spears on a neatly folded white table napkin.

And if you wonder about the number of quail's eggs given in the recipe it is because they often come in boxes of eighteen.

INGREDIENTS

2 kg (4 lbs) **white asparagus**
1 lt (2 pts; 1 qt) **water**
¼ tsp. salt
¼ tsp. sugar

18 **quail's eggs**
250 g (½ lb) **sliced boiled ham**
100 g (3 oz; ½ cup) **butter**

PREPARATION

- Peel the asparagus from the tip down and cut off the woody ends. Cover the spears with cold water and set aside.
- Put the peels and ends with the measured water into a pan, add the salt and sugar; bring to the boil and simmer for 20 minutes.
- Strain this stock and return it to the pan, discard the peels and ends.
- Drain the asparagus spears and add to the stock, bring to the boil

and cook for 10 minutes. Take the pan off the heat, cover and leave for a further 20 minutes.
- Boil the quail's eggs for 5 minutes, rinse in cold water then peel and halve.
- Melt the butter.
- Roll the ham slices.

PRESENTATION
- Lift the asparagus carefully out of the water and transfer immediately to a heated dish.
- Arrange the eggs and ham around the asparagus. The potatoes could be added or served separately.
- Serve the melted butter separately.

Nieuwe Aardappeltjes – New Potatoes

For the following recipe use any variety of tiny new potato – in The Netherlands they are all called *krieltjes* and most greengrocers sell them to you scrubbed and ready for the pot. When boiling any young potato or vegetable, other than the leafy varieties, cook them until they are almost done, then drain and leave them on the side with the pan covered to finish their cooking.

INGREDIENTS
750 g (1½ lbs) new potatoes
salt
4 sprigs parsley

PREPARATION
- Scrub the potatoes and put them into a pan of salted water; bring to the boil, cover the pan and boil until tender. Turn off the heat, drain; put the lid back on and leave to stand until ready to serve.

PRESENTATION
- Chop the parsley and sprinkle over the potatoes just before serving.

One potato, two potatoes, (always) three potatoes more...

There was a time when the 'tuberous nightshade', more commonly called potato, was feared and even cursed as an evil food – the devil's apple. In The Netherlands at the beginning of the 17th century it was one Petrus Hondius, who when not attending to his priestly duties, was experimenting in his garden with extraordinary vegetables and plants, and one of his interesting cultures was the potato, as yet unknown in these parts. By the end of the century, as a result of Hondius' earlier efforts, the potato had supplanted the traditional cereals and many families were eating potatoes at all three main meals of the day. Even the nobility took to the tuber; and so it became *de aardappel* – the apple of the earth.

Today, seed, starch, and ware potatoes (which one buys for home consumption) are the most important arable crops for Dutch farmers and they are grown throughout the country. Varieties are constantly being tried on the market, in the hope, so say the farmers, of finding The Perfect Product; in the meantime it is not a little confusing for the novice to differentiate (there are currently over 150 recognized varieties in The Netherlands).

The best known Dutch potato is the *Bintje*. There is a nice story to go with this name: a Frisian schoolmaster had also become a potato expert and he was constantly breeding new hybrids in his schoolroom laboratory; as each new strain was officially approved he named it after one of his children – he had nine offspring. When he produced the tenth potato he had a naming problem; eventually he called it after his star pupil – *Bintje Jansma*.

The *Bintje* remains the most versatile potato on the Dutch market and is generally available throughout the year. The *Eigenheimer* and the red-skinned *Irene* are good floury potatoes and if you want a particularly tasty potato look for the *Opperdoezer*, though it is only available for a few months in the summer. It is grown in the small town of that name in the north of Holland, you can recognize it by its very irregular shape and thin skin.

Citroentaart met Aardbeien – Lemon Tart with Strawberries

In May the local strawberries are just coming in, though there is an increasingly expanded 'season' due to imports from sunnier climes. The filling for this tart has a lovely lemony tang. Use *umer* if it is available; this is a relatively new Dutch dairy product, it tastes and looks rather like a thick natural yoghurt (which you could use instead), but it is less sharp. If you do substitute yoghurt for the *umer* in a cooked recipe, as in this one which follows, blend in 1 heaped teaspoonful of cornflour to each 150 g (5 oz; ½ cup + 2 tbsp.) yoghurt – this will prevent the yoghurt from separating.

Anneke cooks this tart recipe in a rectangular tin which she says makes for easier serving; our recipe here uses a standard round tin. For a more old-fashioned touch garnish the tart with a few fragrant lemon verbena leaves instead of the mint.

INGREDIENTS *for a 24 cm (10 inch) loose-bottomed flan tin*

For the pastry
>   **75 g** (2 ½ oz; ⅓ cup) **softened butter**
>   **50 g** (2 oz; ¼ cup) **sugar**
>   **1 egg**
>   **150 g** (5 oz; 1 cup) **plain flour**
>   **a pinch of salt**

For the filling
>   **1 lemon**
>   **2 eggs**
>   **150 g** (5 oz; ½ cup + 2 tbsp.) *umer*
>   **100 g** (3 oz; ½ cup) **castor sugar**

>   **250 g** (½ cup) **strawberries**
>   **3 tbsp. redcurrant jelly**
>   **a few sprigs of mint**

- *To make the pastry base:* Cream the butter and sugar; add the egg and beat thoroughly.
- Sieve the flour and salt onto the egg mixture.
- Mix until it forms a ball, cover and leave to rest in a cool place for about 30 minutes.
- Preheat the oven to 200°C /390°F.
- On a floured surface roll out the pastry to line the base and sides of the tin. Leave to rest for a further 15 minutes.
- Bake the pastry 'blind' for about 15 minutes or until lightly coloured.
- Remove the pastry case from the oven and leave to cool. Turn the oven down to 175°C /350°F.

- *To make the filling:* Grate and juice the lemon.
- Beat the eggs, *umer* and sugar until smooth.
- Mix in the lemon zest and juice.
- Pour the filling into the precooked pastry case and bake for 20 minutes.
- Cool to room temperature.
- Hull and halve the strawberries.

PRESENTATION

- When the tart is cool, remove from the tin and put onto a serving platter.
- Arrange the strawberries over the top.
- Melt the redcurrant jelly and brush over the strawberries.
- Garnish with a few mint leaves.

Art and the Family Meal

Luncheon – little has changed down the years

A stranger wanders along a leafy street, his coat blown by a blustery wind which carries more than a hint of rain. For the moment the sun, just past its midday height, has found a gap in the clouds and shines through brightly. The sound of music comes from a nearby house and as the stranger edges closer, drawn by the noisy conviviality, he picks up the melody being tried by several musicians – there is a fiddle… one… no, two…, and pipes – but it must be said the playing is not all that harmonious. And further… could it be… that there is a singing dog in there too?

A young lad leans into the room through the open window puffing deep draughts from a long clay pipe. There is so much music and laughter within that our stranger can peek in unobserved. Round the dining table three generations are gathered. The master of the house, his cap somewhat askew, sits in a handsome wooden chair, the seat of richly studded leather. He has laid aside his fiddling bow for the moment and holding his wine glass high, eyes tight shut in concentration, he joins his womenfolk in lusty song. These two women lead the singing from a well worn script, while a jolly baby beats the tempo from the younger's arms. Who could resist the gaiety?

The room is well appointed, a frieze of tiles rises from the neat laid floor. Over the cupboard is a vase of dried flowers and the sun glints on the workings of a pewter mortar dish. The table is overlaid with a rich woven carpet which is protected against the crumbs by a damask cloth.

The stranger can tell from the smiling faces that a meal has been enjoyed, and there is still ham enough and cheese too; and was it perhaps a dish of eggs that the lady of the house had earlier prepared?

But wait, could it be that there is a note of censure due, has this family perhaps eaten and imbibed just too well? And in the foreground there, is that more wine being poured for the velvet-gowned toddler? Should that youngster really be inhaling the tobacco weed? Where is that housewife's pride – dishes and cracked shells upon the floor?

There on the mantle hangs a written clue, a proverb, the stranger can read it well –
   '*soo d'oude songen, pypen de jonge*'
   … as the old sing, so pipe the young…

Have you guessed? Yes, this is a luncheon scene painted by the 17th century Dutch painter from Leiden, Jan Steen, it is called 'The Merry Family'. Steen was a master of what was to become known as 'genre' painting. He often took his brushes and his canvases into the heart of middle-class homes, not infrequently his own. He painted with simplicity and realism, nor were they just decorative paintings, for if the demeanour of the subjects seems somewhat exaggerated it was because most of his tableaux carried a message which his contemporaries well understood – for us today it is more abstruse. In the family gathering here described, Steen leaves us in no doubt as to his message, it is written there on the canvas: an admonition to parents to set a good example to their young.

Steen's everyday pictures give us an insight into Dutch family life four centuries ago; a voyeurism not found in the grand classical canvases of his forbears, and what can we conclude? For our purposes, perhaps, it is that in truth the Steen lunch is not that dissimilar to what is laid out in the majority of Dutch living rooms today. The tables are still covered by patterned carpets, solid wooden furniture is still in fashion and most lunch-time repasts are of bread and cheese and cold meat, with perhaps an egg dish. Maybe though, we have taken to heart some of the lessons, for milk, not wine, is more likely to fill our drinking glasses, while every single puff of tobacco carries a health warning.

Also painting his neighbourhood families at table was the 19th century painter Van Gogh; his 'Potato Eaters', though it has never been truly admired by his fellow nationals, is now world famous. In this painting, a peasant group of Brabant farmers are gathered for their main meal of the day, there is nothing to eat at this table but one large dish of steaming boiled potatoes and tiny cups of chicory to drink, real coffee for these simple folk would have been an undreamt of luxury.

Earthy perhaps, dark and sombre as this painting is, we know from his letters that Van Gogh did not intend to malign his peasants, but to show them as representing the real values of rural life. He admired the hardworking family unit and their simple togetherness.

And potatoes? Well, they were, and still are an integral part of the Dutch family meal. Ask 'What's for dinner?' and the reply could be 'beans and mince', or 'carrot and chicken'; that there will be potatoes, which are not considered a vegetable, goes without saying.

Een Feestelijke Koffietafel

~

There are times when family and friends gather to celebrate at midday – a graduation, a wedding or the like and on these occasions the meal is elevated to the status of *een koffietafel* – a coffee table. There may be a soup, undoubtedly salads and for today's increasingly ventursome cooks it is likely to become more of a festive brunch – though closer to lunch than to breakfast; that is what Anneke offers us here.

After offering your guests a glass of punch, set the rest out buffet-style with the roulade as the centrepiece.

Vruchtenbowl – Fruit Punch

~

Soep van Wortel en Tomaat – Carrot and Tomato Soup

Bierbrood – Beer Bread

Knapperige Groentesalade – Crunchy Vegetable Salad

Galantine van Kalkoenfilet – Turkey Galantine

Eierrol met Hollandse Garnaaltjes – Dutch Shrimp Roulade

~

Vlierbloesem Pudding – Elderflower Pudding

Gepocheerde Abrikozen – Poached Apricots

Vruchtenbowl – Fruit Punch

This fruit punch is an old Dutch recipe; you can make a non-alcholic version with fizzy lemonade instead of wine. Any combination of fruits can be used depending on their availability in the market and these days we seem to have a wide selection of fresh fruit all the year round.

INGREDIENTS

0.75 lt bottle of dry white wine (1½ pts; 3 cups)
0.75 lt bottle of soda water (1½ pts; 3 cups)
250 g (½ lb) redcurrants
500 g (1 lb) strawberries
250 g (½ lb) raspberries
250 g (½ lb) cherries
1 lime
100 g (3 oz; ½cup) sugar
a few sprigs of mint

PREPARATION

- Chill the bottles of wine and soda.
- Prepare all the soft fruits, slice strawberries and cut stoned cherries in half.
- Grate and juice the lime.
- Mix the fruit, lime zest, lime juice and sugar.
- Reserve some of the mint for garnish. Chop the remaining leaves and add to the fruit.
- Cover and leave to marinade for 1 hour in a cool place.

PRESENTATION

- Just before serving, put fruit, wine and soda into a punch bowl, stir gently.
- Serve in wide glasses, with small spoons to scoop out the fruit.
- Garnish with a little mint.

Soep van Wortel en Tomaat – Carrot and Tomato Soup

Ingredients:
- **250 g** (½ lb) **carrots**
- **500 g** (1 lb) **tomatoes**
- **100 g** (4 oz; ¼ cup) **leeks**
- **2 cm** (¾ inch) **fresh root ginger**
- **1 orange**
- **1 tbsp. oil**
- **1 lt** (2 pts; 1 qt) **chicken stock**
- **1 tsp. honey**
- **salt and freshly ground black pepper**
- **fresh coriander**

PREPARATION
- Peel and slice the carrots.
- Peel and remove seeds from the tomatoes; set one aside for garnish, chop the remainder; slice and wash the leek; peel and grate the ginger.
- Cut a generous strip of rind from the orange; juice the orange.
- Gently fry all the vegetables, ginger and orange peel in the oil until soft. Add the stock and orange juice, bring to the boil and cook until tender.
- Discard the orange peel.
- Purée all the ingredients.
- Season with salt and pepper.
- Cut the reserved tomato into small pieces

PRESENTATION
- Serve the soup hot or cold. Garnish with tomato pieces and coriander leaves.

Bierbrood – Beer Bread

Wholemeal flours have, until recently been the preserve of the Dutch health food shop – *Reformhuis* – or the equivalent market stall; however, they are increasingly to be found on the supermarket shelves. Today's housewife is taking an even more critical look at what she sets before her family and has returned to the homebaking traditions of her great-grandmother's day.

INGREDIENTS

30 g (1 oz) baker's yeast or 2 tsp. dried yeast
50 ml (1½ fl oz; ¼ cup) water
250 ml (½ pt; 1 cup) beer
2 tbsp. molasses
300 g (10 oz; 2 cups) white flour
100 g (3 oz; ⅔ cup) wholemeal flour
100 g (3 oz; ⅔ cup) rye flour
1 tsp. salt

PREPARATION

- Dissolve the yeast in the water.
- Mix the beer with the molasses.
- Mix the 3 flours with the salt, make a well in the middle, pour in the dissolved yeast and work into a third of the flour.
- Add the beer and molasses and knead into a smooth and elastic ball.
- Cover the dough and leave until it has doubled in volume.
- Punch the air out of the dough and form into a round loaf. Cover and leave to prove until it has again doubled in volume.
- Preheat the oven to 225°C/440°F.
- Transfer the loaf to a lightly greased baking sheet and with a sharp knife make deep diagonal cuts across the top.
- Bake for 30 minutes, reduce heat to 175°C/350°F and bake for a further 20 minutes.
- Cool on a wire rack before slicing.

Knapperige Groentesalade – Crunchy Vegetable Salad

Here is a puzzle for you – what do: snow peas (US), mangetout (UK), sugar peas (US), snap peas (US), *pois sucre* (FR), and *peultjes* (NL) all have in common? Answer: they are all the same pea, though there are two varieties: flat-podded and round-podded; the latter, usually called sugar-snaps, have come onto the market in The Netherlands very recently. Both are eaten whole, just top and tail and cook for the minimum of time in the minimum of water.

In choosing the vegetables for this salad look for a contrast of colour and those which are as young and fresh as you can find.

INGREDIENTS

> **500 g (1 lb) mixed vegetables eg. carrots, courgettes (zucchini), celery, mangetout, cauliflower florets**
> **1 sweet red pepper**
> **4 tbsp. oil**
> **juice of ½ a lemon**
> **1 tsp. tomato purée**
> **125 ml (¼ pt; ½ cup) white wine**
> **1 large tomato**
> **1 spring onion**
> **salt and freshly ground black pepper**

For the bouquet garni, to be tied in a piece of cheesecloth
> **½ tsp. thyme**
> **1 bay leaf**
> **1 tsp. coriander seed**
> **a clove garlic**

PREPARATION

- Cut carrots in half lengthwise; cut courgette and celery into strips – all approximately the same length; top and tail mangetout and cut florets from the cauliflower.
- Remove the seeds and membrane from the red pepper and cut into strips.

- Gently fry the vegetables in the oil for 10 minutes.
- Mix the lemon juice, tomato purée and wine; add to the vegetables with the bouquet garni.
- Cover the pan and simmer for another 10 minutes or until the vegetables are just tender.
- Remove from the heat; transfer to a serving bowl.
- Peel, halve and remove seeds from the tomato; slice.
- Slice the spring onion and add to the vegetables with the tomato.
- Season with salt and pepper to taste.
- Remove bouquet garni squeezing out all the moisture.
- Allow to cool.

Galantine van Kalkoenfilet – Turkey Galantine

This recipe could also be served as a hot main meal dish, though extra meat might be needed for hungry diners.

INGREDIENTS
750 g (1 ½ lbs) **boned turkey breast**

For the stuffing
1 tbsp. pistachio nuts
1 shallot
a clove of garlic
25 g (1 oz) bacon
a few sprigs of tarragon
100 g (3 oz) calf's liver sausage
1 tbsp. sherry
salt and freshly ground black pepper
1 tsp. gelatine

PREPARATION
- Trim and butterfly the turkey breast. Reserve the trimmings.
- Preheat the oven to 175°C /350°F.
- Toast the pistachio nuts in the oven while it is preheating.

- *To make the stuffing:* Peel and finely chop the shallot and garlic; chop the turkey trimmings and bacon.
- Reserve some of the tarragon for garnish and snip the remainder.
- Coarsely chop the nuts.
- Mix all these with the liver sausage and sherry.

- Lay the prepared turkey on a large piece of foil.
- Season with salt and pepper.
- Put the stuffing onto one half of the meat, fold over the other half and season the outside. Bring up the foil on both sides and close up making a tight roll.
- Place on a roasting rack and bake in the oven for 1 hour.
- In a small pan sprinkle the gelatine onto a tablespoon of water, leave for 1 minute, then dissolve over a low heat.
- Remove the roll from the oven; carefully open one end of the foil and pour the juices into the dissolved gelatine. Close the foil again and leave the roll to cool.
- Cool the gelatine for about 30 minutes until just beginning to set.

PRESENTATION

- Slice the galantine and arrange on a serving platter; glaze the slices with the gelatine.
- Or allow the gelatine to set completely, then cut into small pieces and sprinkle over the turkey slices.

Eierrol met Hollandse Garnaaltjes – Dutch Shrimp Roulade

For the roulade filling use the tiny Dutch shrimps – they come cooked and peeled and are of a slightly greyish pink colour. Apart from their delicious flavour they are easy to roll into the sponge. (See May for note on *umer* page 84)

INGREDIENTS *for a 20 × 25 cm (8 × 10 inch) baking sheet*

For the roulade
   50 g (2 oz; 3 tbsp.) **butter**
   50 g (2 oz; ⅓ cup) **plain flour**
   300 ml (10 fl oz; 1¼ cups) **milk**
   salt and freshly ground black pepper
   4 eggs
   50 g (2 oz; ½ cup) **grated cheese (mature Gouda)**

For the filling
   250 g (½ lb) **cooked shrimps**
   1 tsp. lemon juice
   a pinch cayenne pepper
   100 g (3 oz) **cream cheese**
   125 ml (¼ pt; ½ cup) ***umer***
   1 tbsp. chives
   1 tsp. grated orange zest

For the garnish
   lemon slices

PREPARATION
- *To make the roulade base:* Grease the baking sheet and line with greaseproof paper.
- Preheat the oven to 200°C / 390°F.
- Melt the butter in a small pan, stir in the flour and cook for a few minutes. Add the milk and continue stirring; bring to the boil and cook until the mixture thickens.
- Season with salt and pepper.
- Transfer to a large bowl and cool slightly.

- Separate the eggs.
- Beating thoroughly, add the yolks to the sauce one at a time, then add the cheese.
- Whisk the egg whites until stiff and fold them into the sauce.
- Transfer the mixture to the prepared baking sheet spreading it evenly.
- Bake for 25 minutes or until golden brown.
- Turn the cooked roulade base onto a second piece of greaseproof paper, peel off the bottom piece.

- *To make the filling:* Mix the shrimps with the lemon juice and chilli pepper.
- Beat the cream cheese with the *umer,* snip the chives and add with the orange zest.
- Fold in the shrimps and season to taste.
- Spread the shrimp mixture over the roulade base.
- Using the greaseproof paper as an aid, roll lengthwise.

PRESENTATION
- Transfer to a long serving platter and slice.
- Garnish with lemon slices.

Vlierbloesem Pudding – Elderflower Pudding

The elderbush grows wild in woods and untamed places throughout Europe. In folklore it is most often associated with witches and spirits from other worlds; for instance, the bush if grown near your front door is said to repell ghosts; on a more practical note, it will keep the flies at bay during the summer months; and if you are still not convinced of its good qualities, it is well known that the elder sited near the house will ward off persistent head colds and coughs.

The flowers, which bloom in June, were often used to flavour pancakes, and clusters were dried for use later in the year. Anneke uses them here to both flavour and decorate this pretty pudding. The deep blue berries which weigh the branches down in September are even more commonly used in jams and wines. Here in The Netherlands a seven week old elderbrandy, if drunk with a little sugar, has been considered a cure for many ills; and even if you are not feeling ill, mix a tablespoon of elderflower syrup with sparkling wine as a pre-dinner cocktail.

In the absence of any elder bushes in your neighbourhood, use the following as a substitute for the dessert syrup: 3 tablespoons of orange flavour liqueur or liqueur from any exotic bottle you have hidden at the back of your cocktail cabinet, to which add 100 ml (3 fl oz; 1/2 cup) water.

INGREDIENTS *for a 1 lt (2 pt; 1 qt) pudding mould*

For the syrup
   100 g (3 oz; ½ cup) **sugar**
   100 ml (3 fl oz; ½ cup) **water**
   1 tsp. lemon juice
   5 elderflower heads

For the pudding
   2 tsp. powdered gelatine
   2 eggs
   100 ml (3 fl oz; ½ cup) **syrup** (see above)

1 tsp. lemon juice
250 g (½ lb; 1½ cups) **quark**
125 ml (¼ pt; ½ cup) **cream**

PREPARATION

- *To make the syrup:* Bring the sugar and water to the boil, stir continuously until the sugar is dissolved.
- Remove from the heat, add the lemon juice and elderflower heads reserving a few sprigs for decoration.
- Cover and leave to infuse overnight, then strain through a sieve lined with cheesecloth.

- *To make the pudding:* In a small pan sprinkle the gelatine onto 2 tablespoons of the syrup, let it stand for 1 minute then dissolve over low heat.
- Separate the eggs.
- Beat the yolks with the remaining elderflower syrup until light and pale yellow.
- Add the dissolved gelatine, lemon juice and quark, beating thoroughly.
- Whisk the egg whites until stiff.
- Whip the cream until thick.
- First fold the egg whites, then the cream into the yolk mixture.
- Pour into the mould which has been rinsed in cold water, cover and chill until set.

PRESENTATION

- Unmould the pudding onto a serving dish and surround with the poached apricots. (recipe follows)
- Decorate with a few sprigs of elderflower blooms.

Gepocheerde Abrikozen – Poached Apricots

Two flavour enhancing tips:
- To give the poached apricots even more flavour, shell and peel a couple of the apricot stones and add the softer inner kernel to the fruit as you cook it, they are good to eat too.
- When you have removed the vanilla pod from the apricot syrup, do not throw it away, but rinse, and when dry pop it into your icing sugar jar to make your own vanilla sugar.

INGREDIENTS

125 ml (4 fl oz; ½ cup) **white wine**
100 g (3 oz; ½ cup) **sugar**
750 g (1 ½ lbs) **fresh apricots**
½ **vanilla pod**

PREPARATION

- Bring the wine and sugar to the boil, stirring all the time until the sugar has dissolved.
- Halve and stone the apricots. Remove the outer shell from some of the stones and peel the kernels (see note above), add with the apricots and vanilla pod to the syrup and simmer for about 15 minutes or until the apricots are just tender.
- Remove vanilla pod and kernels.
- Transfer to a serving bowl, cover and cool.

De koffiemaaltijd

A Dutch luncheon is usually called a *twaalfuurtje*, a twelve o'clock snack, or *koffiemaaltijd*, which literally means a coffee meal. Why such a name I have yet to find the answer, as most people prefer a glass of milk, *karnemelk* – smooth buttermilk or yoghurt, and not coffee at all! This meal has changed little since Jan Steen's time. There are plates of wafer thin slices of cooked meats, cheese, a jar or two of pickles, plus a variety of breads and breadrolls. Bread is bought daily and is sliced while you wait in the bakers; and it is best to get there before midday as very often the day's batch is sold out early.

One particularly Dutch custom which takes some getting used to is that of eating everything, including *belegde broodjes* – filled rolls or sandwiches, with a knife and fork. In some regions there may be eggs on offer for lunch, or different kinds of spiced or fruit bread and in the winter months a warming soup.

If you are in a café at lunchtime there is bound to be an *uitsmijter* on the menu – two open slices of white bread are covered with cold meat (usually ham or roast beef) and cheese, and on top a couple or even three, hot fried eggs; pickled garnish completes the dish. The English translation of this substantial snack is 'bouncer', and it is certainly muscle-building stuff!

The IJssel Lake, Now and Then

A mixed history – the IJsselmeer and its quaint settlements

It was a lake then, in Roman times – Lake Flevo; just some fisherfolk living on its remote marshy banks eking out a fragile existence as the water levels threatened with every high tide. Then in the year 1283 nature took a hand and the whole shape of this region was transformed by a violent storm; many of the waterside hamlets disappeared, as did the lake's natural defences against the sea, it was now open to the even more precarious vagaries of the North Sea winds and salty tides. A lake no more, it became the 'Sea of the South' the *Zuiderzee*.

As its history unfolds, it may seem that that particular northerly wind was the making of the *Zuiderzee's* harbours and ports. There was now access, through the narrow sandbanked channels for the burgeoning trade with the Baltic countries. Ships came and went from ports becoming prominent on the eastern shore, and later came the great tall-masted ships heading for the capital Amsterdam with their precious cargoes of spices from the Orient. In Edam and Muiden shipbuilders hammered and spliced on tall ships and small, while the fishing fleets from Volendam and Urk, Marken and Huizen hauled in large catches of salty herring and anchovy from the rich waters. The glow of those great trading partnerships, the Hanseatic League and later the East India Company, can still be seen on many a fine façade along the waterfronts from Monnikendam to Kampen.

The spin-offs enriched the whole area, not just in wealth but in foreign influences too, spices and citrus fruits, coffees and teas brought new flavours to daily life. In Hindelopen, sea captains wiling away the winter months, decorated their household furniture with colours and patterns seen in the bazaars of the Far East; the craftsmen of that town carry on the tradition to this day. Hoorn was a place from where seafaring dreams came true, it was home to Abel Janszoon Tasman, the famous navigator who discovered Tasmania and New Zealand in 1643, and though maybe not so well know by name, Isaac le Maire. Thirty years earlier with Willem Schouten, he had rounded the very southern-most point of Tierra del Fuego, which they christened after their home port – *Kaap Hoorn.*

Nor was activity all for trade; great naval battles too were fought on the waters of the *Zuiderzee* and when the Spanish rule was finally being rejected it was the northern city of Enkhuizen which was the first to raise the flag of William of Orange.

But the cycle went on and a more direct shipping route to Amsterdam was opened; as the shifting sandbanks made navigation increasingly difficult so the *Zuiderzee* route was no longer viable; the towns and cities were gradually deprived of their shipping levies, lighterage and ship-building businesses and they fell into decline.

In the year 1873, a certain French sailing enthusiast, Henri Havard, set sail to explore '…the perilous waters of the Zuyder Zee,' and to discover for himself '…the ancient capitals of Medomblik and Stavoren before the grass and weeds have totally effaced their walls, and before their names arc definitively erased from the map of Holland.' His book *Dead Cities of the Zuyder Zee* is an oft quoted classic.

Indeed, Henri Havard's predictions may have come true were it not for one Cornelis Lely who launched a scheme, first made public at the end of the 19th century, to enclose that sea again. Once the water could be controlled, he argued, so new land could be drained and developed – there was a chronic shortage of good ground for agriculture, and a dire need for alternative housing for the inhabitants of overcrowded Amsterdam. The plan lay dormant during the 1914-18 conflict but was under way soon after, and in 1932 the last gap in the *Afsluitdijk* was closed. A lake once more, it was renamed the IJsselmeer and work began on draining what was to become the twelfth province of The Netherlands – *Flevoland.*

The IJsselmeer now has an area of 200,000 hectares enclosed by 130 miles of shoreline, most of which is accessible on foot, bicycle or even motor vehicle. The waters of the lake still reach the harbour walls of some 19 villages and towns; and though few of the inhabitants find a livelihood from the sea, many have turned to welcoming the seafaring or landlubber tourist to their picturesque quaysides. There is an air of prosperity once more around this historic waterway.

Nor is the seafaring past forgotten, for dominant on today's seascape are the majestic brown-sailed clippers and barges which ply these waters as of old; rescued from oblivion over the past ten years they have been restored and put back into service; there are over four hundred of them now, ranging in size from about 16 to 36 metres. Their cargos have changed, for it is groups of visitors who book passage on the ships of the past, groups from highrise industrial cities all over Europe. They find release and exhilaration in working by hand the heavy spars and sails of these fine traditional ships.

And if all the sightseeing and history gets too much for you, find a seat in the window of a waterfront café where *de koffie is altijd klaar* – the coffee is always ready, and indulge in a slice of *appelgebak met slagroom* – Dutch apple pie with a confection of cream whirled on top and watch the life of the IJsselmeer unfold around you. (If you are reading this far from The Netherlands, perhaps it will encourage you to come and visit soon... or you could try Anneke's recipe for the apple tart. (see April page 59)

Dinner Al Fresco

Summer is such an uncertain season in this part of the world
that one does hesitate somewhat in suggesting that the table
could be laid out of doors and the barbeque lit up for a
dinner 'al fresco'. Excuse the use of the Italian in our Dutch
book, but Italian foods and restaurants are probably the
most popular foreign imports in The Netherlands at present,
after the Indonesians of course. Theirs is an influence that
has brought the flavours and tastes of the sunny South to
every town centre in The Netherlands.

However, let us hope for fine weather and if the worst comes
to the worst on the night of your summer dinner, well, you
can just as easily put the chops under the grill.

Volkorenbrood met Tuinkruiden – Herbed Wholewheat Bread

Salade van Gerookte Eendeborst met Zomervruchten
Salad of Smoked Breast of Duck with Summer Fruit

Schouderkarbonade op de Barbeque
Barbequed Pork Shoulder Chops

Salade van Zilvervliesrijst met Kerrie
Curried Brown Rice Salad

Gemengde Bonensalade met Knoflookcroutons
Mixed Bean Salad with Garlic Croutons

Watermeloen Sorbet – Watermelon Sorbet

Amandelkrullen – Almond Tuiles

Volkorenbrood met Tuinkruiden
Herbed Wholewheat Bread

This bread makes much use of herbs, it is best to use a combination of what fresh ones you can find, or which perhaps grow in your window boxes or herb garden. (If you have run out of time for kneading and rising… don't tell Anneke… just chop the herbs finely, mix into some softened butter and use to transform a 'french loaf': slice the bread, not quite through, sandwich with the herbed butter, wrap in foil and heat through before serving. Many Dutch restaurants offer herbed butter, as an alternative to garlic, with the dinner bread.)

INGREDIENTS
2 shallots
50 g (2 oz; 3 tbsp.) butter
4 tbsp. chopped fresh herbs (any selection as available)
20 g (⅔ oz) baker's yeast or 1½ tsp. dried yeast
1 tsp. honey
250 ml (½ pt; 1 cup) water
150 g (5 oz; 1 cup) wholewheat flour
250 g (½ lb; 1 ⅔ cups) plain flour
1 tsp. salt

PREPARATION
- Chop the shallots and gently fry in the butter until soft. Cool.
- Chop the herbs.
- Dissolve the yeast with the honey in the water.
- Mix the two flours and salt in a large bowl, make a well in the middle, add the dissolved yeast and work into a third of the flour.
- Add the herbs and the shallots with any remaining butter from the pan.
- Knead into a smooth and elastic ball.
- Cover and leave until it has doubled in volume.
- Punch the air out of the dough and press into a rectangle; then roll up tightly, tucking in the ends.
- Transfer to a lightly greased baking sheet, flatten the loaf slightly

and make a few diagonal cuts across the top.
- Cover and leave to prove until it has again doubled in volume.
- Preheat the oven to 200°C /390°F.
- Bake for 30 minutes; lower heat to 175°C /350°F and bake for a further 10 minutes.
- Cool on a wire rack.

Salade van Gerookte Eendborst met Zomervruchten
Salad of Smoked Breast of Duck with Summer Fruit

Anneke challenges us somewhat with her July salads as there is hardly a lettuce among them, except for a few decorative leaves. This colourful salad is a subtle blend of sweet and savoury, epitomized in the honey mustard. If this is not available you can make your own by mixing a little honey with a grainy mustard of your choice.

INGREDIENTS

For the sauce
1 egg
2 tbsp. sugar
2 tbsp. lime juice
1 tbsp. honey mustard
125 ml (¼ pt; ½ cup) cream
salt and freshly ground black pepper

For the salad
50 g (2 oz; ⅔ cup) flaked almonds
1 smoked fillet of duck (approximately 300 g; 12 oz)
250 g (½ lb) raspberries
3 peaches
a few decorative lettuce leaves.

- *To make the sauce:* Separate the egg.
- In a small pan stir the yolk, sugar, lime juice and mustard over a low heat until creamy. Cool.
- Whisk the egg white.
- Whip the cream until it holds soft peaks, fold carefully into the yolk mixture with the egg white.
- Season with salt and pepper and set aside.

- In a small pan toast the almonds over a low heat.
- Remove the layer of fat from the duck fillet and cut this into very thin strips.
- Fry these strips over low heat until the fat has been rendered and the strips are crisp. Drain on kitchen paper; reserve the fat for use on another occasion.
- Cut the fillet across into thin slices.
- Prepare the raspberries.
- Skin and halve the peaches, discard the stones; cut the peaches into thin slices.
- Wash and dry the lettuce leaves.

PRESENTATION

- Arrange the lettuce on the dinner plates, then the duck and fruit.
- Spoon some of the sauce over the duck. Sprinkle with the almonds and crispy bacon strips.
- Serve the rest of the sauce separately.

Schouderkarbonade op de Barbeque
Barbequed Pork Shoulder Chops

INGREDIENTS

For the sauce
- 1 red chilli pepper
- 1 shallot
- a clove of garlic
- 1 tsp. grainy mustard
- 1 tsp. prepared horseradish
- 2 tbsp. lemon juice
- 2 tbsp. brown sugar
- 1 tsp.salt
- 50 g (2 oz; 3 tbsp.) butter
- 125 ml (¼ pt; ½ cup) tomato ketchup
- 1 tbsp. Worcestershire sauce
- 125 ml (¼ pt; ½ cup) water

4 thick pork shoulder chops

PREPARATION
- Remove the seeds from the chilli pepper, peel the garlic and shallot, then chop very finely.
- Put these and all the other ingredients for the sauce into a pan, bring to the boil and simmer uncovered for about 15 minutes.
- Remove from the heat and cool.
- Brush the chops with the sauce and grill or barbeque for about 20 minutes or until well done. Turn frequently and baste with the sauce when turning.

PRESENTATION
- Serve the remaining sauce with the chops.

Salade van Zilvervliesrijst met Kerrie
Curried Brown Rice Salad

Brown rice is less refined than white, and requires more cooking time than other varieties as the grains still have their bran coating; it is this outer layer which gives the rice its characteristic nutty flavour. Rice mixed with a dressing while still warm really absorbs the spices, here a mixture of curry and ginger. The ginger syrup can be bought in jars, or use a spoonful from that jar of preserved ginger.

INGREDIENTS
> 300 ml (10 oz; 1½ cups) **brown rice**
> 500 ml (1 pt; 2 cups) **water**

For the dressing
> a **clove of garlic**
> 1 tbsp. **wine vinegar**
> 1 tbsp. **lemon juice**
> 1 tbsp. **ginger syrup**
> 1 tsp. **curry powder**
> ¼ tsp. **chilli powder**
> **salt and freshly ground black pepper**
> 100 ml (6 tbsp.) **sunflower oil**
> 1 **green pepper**
> 1 **red pepper**
> 3 **spring onions**
> 50 g (2 oz; ⅓ cup) **raisins**
> a few sprigs of **parsley**

> 2 **tomatoes**

PREPARATION
- Put the rice into a sieve and wash under cold running water until the water runs clear, drain.
- Transfer to a heavy-bottomed pan, add the measured water.
- Bring to the boil and boil uncovered for about 10 minutes or until

most of the water has evaporated.
- Cover and cook gently for a further 20 minutes. Remove from the heat, and let the covered pan stand for about 10 minutes.
- Fluff the rice with a fork and transfer to a bowl.

- *To make the dressing:* Peel and chop the garlic, mix with the wine vinegar, lemon juice, syrup, curry powder, chilli and pepper and salt; blend in the oil.
- Mix the dressing into the rice with a fork. Cool.

- Remove the seeds and membrane from the peppers and cut into small pieces, chop the parsley, slice the spring onions and mix into the rice with the raisins. Slice the tomatoes.

PRESENTATION
- Serve garnished with tomato slices.

Peulvruchten – dried pulses

White beans are one of about eight or nine varieties of pulses which are most common in The Netherlands. Several of these have been grown here for centuries and were staple fare before the advent of the potato. Among the most common are green marrowfat peas which when dried and split are the basic ingredient of *Erwtensoep* – Dutch split pea soup (see February page 30); another traditional winter dish calls for brown beans which are cooked with bacon and syrup. There is one uniquely Dutch pulse, the *kapucijner* or *raasdonder*; these are eaten fresh when they are harvested in the early summer, they have a green or distinctly blue-purple pod, and are filled with plump starchy peas. They are probably best enjoyed when dried, then they turn a light brown colour and as they dry they actually shrivel slightly so they have a wrinkled appearance. These form the basis for 'The Captain's Table' – a naval dish of spiced *kapucijners*, cooked with mustard, onions and bacon and eaten accompanied by dishes of pickled vegetables. All the pulses, except for the split peas and lentils have to be soaked overnight.

Gemengde Bonensalade met Knoflookcroutons
Mixed Bean Salad with Garlic Croutons

This recipe calls for summer savoury – *bonekruid* – the winter variety is similar; this aromatic herb is actually known as the 'bean herb' and most Dutch greengrocers will offer it when you buy fresh broad beans. Do not be too heavy-handed as savoury is quite strong and a little goes a long way. It does retain its flavour well when dried so there is no need for waste. You could use thyme instead.

And from bean herb to the beans themselves, the bean salad calls for both a pulse and the fresh green bean: dried white beans and *sperziebonen* – which are green or French beans and should need little introduction.

INGREDIENTS
    100 g (3 oz; ½ cup) **dried white beans**
    250 g (½ lb) **green beans**
    1 **small red onion**
    a **clove of garlic**
    125 g (4 oz; ½ cup) **celery**
    1 **tomato**
    ½ **cucumber**

For the dressing
    1 tbsp. **lemon juice**
    salt and freshly ground black pepper
    3 tbsp. **oil**
    2 sprigs **summer savoury**

For the croutons
    2 slices **day-old wholewheat bread**
    a **clove of garlic**
    1 tbsp. **oil**

- Soak the dried beans overnight; bring to the boil in the soaking liquid and simmer for 30-40 minutes or until soft.
- Drain and season to taste with salt and pepper. Cool.
- Top and tail the green beans and cut diagonally into 5 cm (2 inch) pieces.
- Cook these beans in a little water in a covered pan for about 10 minutes until just tender. Drain and rinse in cold water.
- Peel and chop the onion and garlic; trim and slice the celery.
- Peel and remove the seeds from the tomato and cut into small pieces.
- Wash the cucumber, halve and slice.

- *To make the dressing:* Mix the lemon juice with the salt and pepper, then blend in the oil.
- Snip the summer savoury into the dressing.
- Put the beans and vegetables into a large bowl and mix in the dressing.

- *To make the croutons:* Remove the crusts from the bread and cut into cubes.
- Halve the garlic, heat in a frying pan with the oil; remove the garlic when light brown; gently fry the bread cubes until golden brown, (about 10 minutes).

PRESENTATION

- Arrange the salad on a serving platter and just before serving sprinkle with croutons.

Watermeloen Sorbet – Watermelon Sorbet

For dessert this month there is an easy sorbet, accompanied by crispy almond tuiles, the fun of these of course is rolling the tuiles, but I am told that practice makes perfect!

There are seedless watermelons on the market now making preparation so much easier. If you buy a whole melon an alternative might be to scoop out some melon balls and set them aside to serve with the sorbet.

INGREDIENTS *for a 1 lt (2 pt; 1 qt) freezer container*
   750 g (1 ½ lbs; 5 cups) **watermelon flesh**
   150 g (5 oz; 1 cup) **sugar**
   1 orange
   1 lime

- Remove the seeds from the watermelon and purée the flesh with the sugar; pass through a sieve.
- Grate then juice the orange and lime and mix into the purée.
- Transfer to a container and freeze for 1 to 2 hours.
- Remove from the freezer and beat vigorously to break down any ice crystals, or purée in a food processor.
- Freeze for a further 2 hours.
- Transfer to the refrigerator for about 15 minutes before serving.

PRESENTATION

- Serve scoops of the sorbet in large wine glasses, accompanied by almond tuiles.

Sweets and sweetmeats

Almonds are in the recipes again this month, but they are not just popular in the kitchen, if you visit any flamboyantly decorated *snoepwinkel* – sweet shop, there will be rows of tall glass-topped jars filled with of one the world's oldest sweetmeats – the sugared almond. Mix these with soft melting *fondants* and fruit jellies and you have a traditional Dutch wedding selection called *bruidsuikers* – the bride's sugars.

Salty sweets – a contradiction in terms, the Dutch love them, so much so that they eat twenty nine million of them a year, but then Tutankhamen found them good too... like to try them? These are called *drop*, licorice sweets. They are made from the dried roots of the 'glycymhiza glabra' plant; these sub-tropical roots are brought to The Netherlands to be pulped, cooked with added ingredients and dried again. Many people like them with their natural taste – *zoute* – a distinctly salty flavour, others prefer the *zoete*, much sweeter. There are almost 70 varieties and it is fun just reading the names: *klompjesdrop* – wooden shoe drops, *hangsnorren* – drooping moustache drops, *sleuteldrop* – key drops, *hondekoppendrop* – are those for dogs? and the colourful English Allsorts are on the list too.

To buy from the tempting displays of chocolates and the 'very moreish' coffee beans (no bean, just pure chocolate shaped to look like one), you need to visit the cake or speciality shop. And one more very special Dutch treat – *Haagsche Hopjes,* these are boiled sweets, coffee flavoured and are so traditional that there is even a *Hopjes* museum... but on with the cooking...

Amandelkrullen – Almond Tuiles

Almonds, though expensive imports, are an integral part of the Dutch bakery world and as almond paste they have found their way into a host of fruit breads and spicy biscuits (see the December recipes). Where you see a *gevulde* biscuit or cake, it simply means 'filled' with an almond core. To get the best quality – and there is quite a range – buy from a reputable baker.

It is best to bake these biscuits in two batches; first, because most ovens are not large enough to fit all at one time, and second, it will give you time to roll the first lot while the others are baking.

INGREDIENTS *for approximately 15 biscuits*

    1 egg white
    60 g (2 oz; ⅓ cup) **castor sugar**
    25 g (1 oz; 2 tbsp.) **plain flour**
    a pinch of salt
    25 g (1 oz; 2 tbsp.) **butter**
    50 g (2 oz; ½ cup) **flaked almonds**

PREPARATION

- Stir the egg white with the sugar until the sugar is dissolved.
- Sieve the flour and salt and thoroughly blend with the egg white.
- Melt the butter and stir into the blended mixture with the almonds.
- Cover and refrigerate for 15 minutes.
- Preheat the oven to 200°C/390°F.
- Grease and flour two baking sheets.
- Drop teaspoonfuls of batter at 10 cm (4 inch) intervals onto one of the baking sheets and flatten each with a fork to give a thin round biscuit.
- Bake for 8-10 minutes until the edges are golden brown.
- Working quickly, remove the biscuits with a spatula, one at a time and press onto a rolling pin for a few seconds until it just begins to hold its shape.
- Repeat the process with the rest of the batter.

The snackbar

It is as a tourist perhaps that one comes to savour the simple tastes of this country, the traditional snacks of the fisherfolk and farmer. In every picturesque centre, never far from the car park or station, there will be a row of food stalls – flags flying, display cabinets full of specialities.

One stall is bound to sell fish – the favourite must be the *maatjes*, the *nieuwe haring* – raw salted herring. Or perhaps you would prefer *gerookte paling* – smoked eel, these wriggly creatures are still fished from the IJsselmeer and are considered a great delicacy; buy them whole for a snack later, or have a *broodje paling* – a filleted eel roll right there. Mussels are very popular and are often sold crisp fried and eaten with a generous dip of mayonnaise.

Not far away there is sure to be a stall selling *patates frites* – French fries and other deep fried savoury treats. It is never the wrong moment for a portion of *frites met...* chips with... it almost goes without saying that for all Dutchmen it is unthinkable to have chips without mayonnaise, or perhaps a spicy *satésaus* – made from peanut butter, popularly called *patatje pinda*.

Kroketten and the more solid *frikandel* are other popular snacks, these are essentially soft-centred rissoles – but watch out – they come straight out of the hot oil and that first bite can be deceptively steamy hot. There are other pastry type snacks – *loempias* for instance, these are Indonesian spring rolls and are filled with vegetables and perhaps chicken, and *kaassoufflés* – pastries with a cheese filling. Though not many stalls sell the ubiquitous hamburger, quite a few have what can best be described as a sort of minced-meat ball, *een gehaktballetje*.

For those with a sweet tooth, look out for the signs saying *poffertjes* – these are tiny pancakes which are fried right before you and served with icing sugar and butter; for a few extra cents you can have your portion flavoured with rum or orange liqueur – delicious!

'Say Cheese'

The Dutch – leaders in cheese production since time immemorial

It is early Friday morning in Alkmaar, in the province of North Holland. Across the market square an army of blue-clad porters is busy setting out some 30,000 kilos of cheese in long orderly lines; there are yellow cartwheels of cheese big and small, these are the Goudas, and over there being scrutinized by a serious group of white-coated officials is a stack of almost round yellow balls which must come from Edam; it is mostly the export cheeses which have a red coating.

The cheeses on display are under close examination, their appearance, colour and flavour are being compared. One of the experts picks a cheese at random, weighs it up and down in his hand, and amazingly, he puts it to his ear, taps it; from the sound he says, he can tell a lot about the texture within, whether it has too many holes or too few, whether the holes are properly distributed. He inserts an instrument like an apple corer, it is called a cheese trier or cheese iron, and with this he withdraws a sample which he smells, and prods, and then pushes back in from where it came. He scribbles some notes which he will file away, to be consulted again at the end of the market season when the winner of the 'Best Cheese Competition' will be announced.

Further on there is a much more heated discussion taking place – a bargaining session is under way; a trier is used to draw out a core of cheese… sniff… um… a price? The two men almost shake on it, but no, just a clap of right hands and they move apart. More discussion and with each clap of hands the price changes, finally with a clasp the deal is done.

Until shortly after the last war, 50–70% of all cheese sold in The

Netherlands changed hands this way, but as demand and production in the creameries has increased so much, it is no longer practical. Today the weekly cheese prices are regulated in Friesland, round a committee table in the city of Leeuwarden. Here in Alkmaar the market is mainly for the benefit of the onlookers, though the old traditions are still practiced among those producing farm cheese near Gouda and Bodegraven.

So back to Alkmaar's market, for gathered round the square now are members of the *Kaasdragers* – the Cheesebearer's Guild. The guild consists of four *vemen* – groups; each consists of seven members and they are distinguishable one from another by their brightly coloured and lacquered boaters. They are otherwise dressed in white and over their shoulders they wear long leather straps for carrying the wooden *berrie* – these are a sort of wooden bier, with long handles but no wheels, used for carrying the cheeses. The leader of the *veem,* called the *tasman* – the bagman, for he wears a special black leather bag, is stationed by the huge scales in the 16th century weigh house ready for action.

At ten on the dot the copper bell rings the start of the market. As the deals are struck, so in pairs the *kaasdragers* literally run into action: 125 kilos of cheese are moved quickly onto a bier, up and off they lope across the square to have the cheese officially weighed, then back again to the waiting transport. All these cheeses must be moved by twelve noon; though in its heyday in the early part of this century, this market often ran until the small hours.

What makes the market so much fun for the thousands of spectators who flock to watch and photograph, is that the bearers are so evidently enjoying themselves. Most have their own businesses or jobs, but once a week for the twenty-two week season from April to the end of October, they clock in at their guild room in the time-honoured way; and woe betide anyone who is late, for that misdemeanour their name will be written on the chalk board and a fine levied!

A nation of *kaaskoppen* – cheeseheads, the Dutch are sometimes rudely called, and there is one oft quoted explanation of the nickname: the ever practial farmers of North Holland when threatened by missiles during riots against the ruling Spanish powers snatched up the empty cheese moulds (the round Edam variety) and shoved them on their heads for protection! But the name is perhaps a kinder reference to the importance given to cheese as an invaluable export rather than just a supply for the family larder.

The Dutch have been exporting cheese for centuries, there are records dating back to the 13th century of bargaining sessions with English and Scottish buyers, and it is known that the bargemen moving along the Rhine regularly paid their tolls in cheese. With the rise of the Hanseatic League at about the same time, cheese was being exported to the Baltic and Mediterranean countries. Today The Netherlands is at the top of the world cheese export league, much of it going to neighbouring Germany.

One of the reasons for the success of the trade is that the shape of the cheeses makes them easy to transport – most are flat cartwheel shapes, and perhaps more important is the fact that these cheeses store extremely well. An Edam cheese was found in the late 1950's somewhere in the Artic wastes having being abandoned by Scott's expedition forty four years earlier, and it was still edible... just!

Know your Dutch cheeses

There are four place names which epitomize Dutch cheese, they are the towns of Edam, Gouda and Leiden, and the province of Friesland. In common, they all produce semi-hard cheeses with a dry rind, but there are marked differences too.

Edam: this has been the best known Dutch cheese abroad and it's round red waxed shape is world famous, though for the home market it comes with a yellow rind. Today, all the Edam cheeses are made in creameries except for one farm in North Holland. They usually come in one kilo (Baby Edam) or two kilo balls. Edam is made from semi-skimmed milk and so has a lower fat content (40%) than the Goudas. At six weeks, when most Edam cheese comes onto the market, it has a mild taste with a smooth texture. Its unique flavour comes – so we are told – from the special properties of the grazing in North Holland.

In my opinion one of the best varieties of Edam is the *Commissiekaas* – called Mimelotte in other countries. This is a deep orange coloured cheese – matured for over six months; for some reason it is difficult to buy here in The Netherlands though it is popular in France and Belgium, and is even made in those countries. Edam cheese also comes spiced with cumin.

Gouda: it is said that the first Gouda variety of cheese was actually made in a neighbouring village, Stolwijk, but whatever the origins, today about 60% of all Dutch cheese production is of the Gouda type. It is a full fat cheese and comes in wheels weighing from half a kilo up to 36 kilos. With these cheeses the bigger the better as the large ones do not dry out as quickly as the small. Most are now made in creameries, but there is a swing back to the old fashioned farmhouse Goudas, free of artificial colouring or preservatives, these have the word *boerenkaas* stamped on the label. The label also gives details of the fat content, a true Gouda must be 48+ which means that the fat is 48% of the dry matter (for those who like the statistics – most of these cheeses average 60% dry to 40% liquid).

There are Gouda cheeses with cumin, herbs, whole black peppercorns, paprika, mustard seed, ginger and a delicious one flecked with nettle leaves.

The quality of the flavour changes from mild to mature according to the age of the cheese:

jong – young, 6-10 weeks old (this is probably the most popular cheese in The Netherlands);

jong belegen – semi matured, 10-14 weeks;

belegen – mature, 4-6 months;

extra belegen – extra mature, 7-10 months old;

oud – aged, 10 months-1 year;

overjarig – any cheese over a year old.

Leiden: the Leiden cheeses when mature are quite sharp, they come with a 20 or 40% fat content and are strongly spiced with cumin, and sometimes caraway seed. The *boerenleidse* – Leiden farmhouse cheese, has a red rind and a different shape from the Goudas, the top is slighly rounded but the bottom edge is more angular and each cheese is marked with the crossed keys of the city of Leiden.

While cheese-making was traditionally the job of the farmer's wife, with the *boerenleidse* the farmer too took a hand, (or should I say 'a foot'?) for when it was time to knead the cumin into the curd, the farmer would roll up his trousers, take his shoes off and literally pound the mixture with his bare feet – no, they don't do that any more, though this cheese is far more popular with the older male generation than the ladies!

Friesland: Friesland and cows are synonomous and while butter has been the province's top priority there is one well known cheese from the region, *Friese nagelkaas* – Frisian clove cheese, this is a firm textured cheese, matured for four months and spiced with cumin and cloves. It is made in wheels of eight kilos.

These are the most famous Dutch cheeses but there are many others: curd cheeses, the creamy Kernhem, cheeses to appeal to the more health conscious with reduced fat or salt content and not forgetting the ewe's cheese which is a speciality of the island of Texel. Finally, the increasingly popular varieties of goat's cheeses; these last come soft, or semi-hard as a mild or mature cheese; goat's cheeses are a real boon for those with milk allergies.

The Dutch eat sliced cheese for breakfast, and invariably for lunch. Slices of Gouda come simply melted over a pancake or maybe as a crispy topping on a dish of vegetables. A regular favourite, *aardappelen met kaas* – is mashed potato with grated cheese melted through and there is a popular winter dish called *kaasdoop* – a mixture of cheese and milk which originated in the farmhouse kitchens. Strangely, cheese did not play any further part in cooked dishes in The Netherlands until recently when advertising and foreign travel have begun to encourage a much wider use.

Fashions and health fads too, come and go, but among the basic foodstuffs still being enjoyed in The Netherlands are 'butter and eggs and a pound of cheese'; and for myself, well I am not ready for a well balanced food pill – not yet!

A Picnic

Anneke has prepared a very grand picnic for us this month and her selection would be suitable for a group of 8-10 people, while any one recipe would be sufficient for 4.

There are two savoury recipes – one fish and one meat; two salads, one with a goat's cheese roll that has an unexpected bite to it and two interesting breads, one fruity and one spicy. Don't forget that to be really Dutch you need a *pikante* – tasty farmhouse Gouda to go with the raisin buns. Finally, to round off, there is an easily transportable fruit flan.

Saucijzebroodjes met Lamsgehakt
Sausage Rolls with Minced Lamb

Quiche van Venkel met Verse Zalm
Fennel Quiche with Fresh Salmon

Rollade van Hollandse Geitekaas met Rode Paprikasalade
Dutch Goat's Cheese Roll with Red Pepper Salad

Aardappelsalade met Gemarineerde Groente
Potato Salad with Marinaded Vegetables

Krentenbollen met Goudse Kaas – Currant Buns with Gouda Cheese

Oudhollandse Peperkoek – Old Dutch Pepper Cake

Limburgse Vlaai – Limburg Flan

Saucijzebroodjes met Lamsgehakt
Sausage Rolls with Minced Lamb

Sausage meat as such you cannot find in The Netherlands, but there is an ever greater selection of sausages – pork, beef, or a mixture of the two; there are veal and turkey sausages, oriental spicy sausages or barbeque ones. In a different category is *worst* – this is a large, finely blended cooked sausage which you will find at the delicatessen counter. There are many varieties and they are sold thinly sliced to be eaten cold with bread and are not to be confused with the *rookworst* which is a smoked sausage; this is usually cooked in soups and stews. When shopping for these sausage rolls, choose a piece of very lean lamb, preferably leg; the shoulder and breast are too fatty. Anneke usually asks her butcher to mince it for her. These lamb rolls are somewhat similar to the large *saucijzebroodjes*, sausage rolls, which you can buy ready made from many outlets.

INGREDIENTS *for 12 rolls*

   250 g (½ lb) puff pastry (fresh or frozen)
   1 egg
   a few mint leaves
   250 g (½ lb) lean minced lamb
   1 tsp. tomato purée
   1 tbsp. grated lemon zest
   salt and freshly ground black pepper

PREPARATION

   • Preheat the oven to 225°C / 440°F.
   • Roll out the (defrosted) pastry to a 3 mm (⅛ inch) thickness and cut into twelve 5 × 10 cm (2 × 4 inch) pieces.
   • Lightly whisk the egg.
   • Chop the mint.
   • Mix together the lamb, mint, tomato purée, lemon zest, half the egg, salt and pepper.
   • Dip your hands in a little flour and shape the lamb mixture into twelve 5 cm (2 inch) sausages which will fit across the pastry

rectangles.
- Put each sausage across the middle of a piece of pastry, dampen the edge and fold the pastry over, pressing down the edges gently with a fork.
- Add a few drops of water to the remaining egg and brush over the rolls.
- Transfer the rolls to a baking sheet which has been sprinkled with a little water.
- Bake for 10-15 minutes, or until golden.
- Cool on a wire rack.

Quiche van Venkel met Verse Zalm
Fennel Quiche with Fresh Salmon

Fennel and salmon compliment each other in this quiche in a very subtle way. Fennel is a relative newcomer to the Dutch greengrocers' shelves, in appearance it is not unlike rounded celery stalks, though the feathery leaves mark it out as being of the same family as dill. It has a stronger aniseed flavour than dill and is excellent either cooked, or as a crunchy salad ingredient, as in this month's potato salad. Use a natural thick yoghurt in place of the *umer* if necessary.
An extra fishy suggestion for the picnic is to serve soft finger rolls filled with smoked eel.

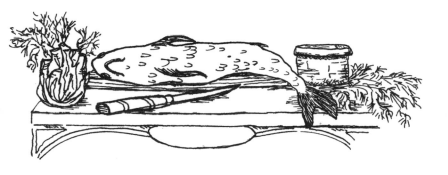

INGREDIENTS *for a 26 cm (11 inch) loose bottomed flan tin*

For the pastry

200 g (7 oz; 1⅓ cups) **plain flour**
a pinch of salt
100 g (3 oz; ⅓ cup + 1 tbsp.) **butter**
1 egg yolk
2 tbsp. water

For the filling

500 g (1 lb) **fennel bulb**
250 g (½ lb) **fillet of salmon**
a few sprigs of dill
175 ml (6 fl oz; ¾ cup) *umer*
125 ml (¼ pt; ½ cup) **cream**
3 eggs
salt and freshly ground black pepper

PREPARATION

- Sieve the flour and salt. Cut the butter into the flour until it resembles coarse breadcrumbs.
- Lightly mix the egg yolk and water; then with a knife quickly mix into the flour, work into a ball; cover and leave to rest in a cool place for an hour.
- Trim and halve the fennel, cut into thin slices.
- Cook in a little water until just tender. Drain well.
- Cut the salmon fillet across into thin strips.
- Preheat the oven to 200°C/390°F.
- Roll out the pastry to fit the base and sides of the flan tin.
- Bake 'blind' for 15 minutes. Remove from the oven.
- Arrange the fennel and the salmon on the pastry base. Snip the dill and sprinkle over the filling.
- Beat together the *umer*, cream, eggs, salt and pepper and pour into the pastry case.
- Put into the hot oven and reduce the temperature to 180°C/360°F.
- Bake the quiche for about 30 minutes or until the filling is set and the top golden.

Rollade van Hollandse Geitekaas met Rode Paprikasalade
Dutch Goat's Cheese with Red Pepper Salad

There is conflict between the Dutch and English language when it comes to peppers; what the English call a sweet pepper or capsicum the Dutch call *paprika*; and the *rode peper* is the English chilli pepper; paprika powder is the same in both languages.

That apart, the Dutch growers have really specialized in the cultivation of peppers and it is one of their most important vegetable exports. There are square and tapered peppers, they do not differ much in taste. Peppers come in all colours, green, yellow, red, purple, black, even orange – these are often on sale near the Queen's birthday in April, in celebration of the House of Orange. The green pepper is usually a little cheaper, but only because it has been picked before it has had time to ripen into one of the other colours.

INGREDIENTS
For the roll
> 150 g (5 oz) **rindless Dutch goat's cheese**
> 50 g (2 oz; 3 tbsp.) **softened butter**
> 60 ml (2 fl oz; ¼ cup) **cream**
> 25 g (1 oz; ¼ cup) **grated cheese** (mature Gouda)
> **a few sprigs of parsley**
> **a clove of garlic**
> 1 tsp. **grated lemon zest**
> **freshly ground pepper**
> **a pinch of cayenne**

For the salad
> **4 red peppers**
> 1 tbsp. **oil**
> 50 g (2 oz; ¼ cup) **black olives – pitted**
> **a few sprigs of parsley**
> 1 tbsp. **lemon juice**

PREPARATION

- Blend the goat's cheese with the butter, cream and grated cheese.
- Finely chop the parsley and the garlic, mix into the cheeses with the lemon zest.
- Season with pepper and cayenne.
- Put the cheese mixture onto a piece of plastic wrap and form into a thick roll.
- Chill for at least an hour.

- Preheat the oven to 225°c/440°f.
- Cut the red peppers in half, remove the seeds and membrane. Brush with the oil and put, cut side down, in an ovenproof dish. Put into the hot oven for 20 minutes or until the skins start to blister.
- Remove from the oven, cover and leave on the side to steam for a further 10 minutes.
- Lift out the peppers, discard the skins which should now pull off easily, cut the peppers into strips and put into a bowl.
- Chop parsley, slice the olives and scatter both over the peppers.
- Season with salt and pepper and sprinkle with the lemon juice.

PRESENTATION

- Cut the cheese roll into thick slices; dipping the knife into hot water before cutting each slice.
- Arrange a circle of cheese slices around the edge of a serving platter, spoon the pepper mixture into the middle.

Aardappelsalade met Gemarineerde Groente
Potato Salad with Marinaded Vegetables

INGREDIENTS

1 green pepper
125 g (4 oz; ½ cup) celery
125 g (4 oz; ½ cup) fennel
2 spring onions
a clove of garlic
1 tbsp. lemon juice
a few sprigs of thyme
a pinch of aniseed
salt and freshly ground black pepper
4 tbsp. oil
500 g (1 lb) new potatoes
a handful of basil leaves
a few decorative lettuce leaves

PREPARATION

- Remove the seeds and membrane from the pepper.
- Trim the celery and fennel; chop into small pieces with the pepper.
- Thinly slice the spring onions; peel and finely chop the garlic.
- Mix the lemon juice, thyme, aniseed, pepper and salt; blend in the oil.
- Marinade all the vegetables in this dressing for a few hours, or overnight.
- Scrub the new potatoes and boil in water to cover, until just cooked; drain.
- Cut the cooked potatoes into slices while still warm and pour the marinaded vegetables over them; tear the basil leaves and mix through.

PRESENTATION

- Arrange the lettuce leaves around a platter, mound the potato salad in the middle.

Krentenbollen met Goudse Kaas
Currant Buns with Gouda Cheese

INGREDIENTS *for 10 rolls*

150 g (5 oz; 1 cup) **currants**
75 g (2½ oz; ½ cup) **raisins**
1 tsp. grated lemon zest
20 g (⅔ oz) **baker's yeast or** 1½ tsp. **dried yeast**
1 tsp. sugar
150 ml (5 fl oz; ½ cup + 2 tbsp.) **milk**
300 g (10 oz; 2 cups) **plain flour**
100 g (3 oz; ⅔ cup) **wholemeal flour**
½ tsp. salt
1 egg
25 g (1 oz; 2 tbsp.) **softened butter**
250 g (½ lb) **sliced cheese** (mild Gouda)

PREPARATION

- Soak the dried fruit in plenty of water for about 20 minutes. Drain and pat dry. Dust with a little flour.
- Mix the lemon zest into the fruit.
- Dissolve the yeast with the sugar in the milk.
- Mix the flours and salt into a bowl, make a well in the middle, pour in the dissolved yeast and work the yeast mixture into a third of the flour.
- Lightly whisk the egg and add half of it and the butter to the flour.
- Knead into a smooth and elastic ball.
- Cover the dough and leave until it has doubled in volume.
- Punch the air out of the dough and press into a rectangle.
- Scatter the dried fruits on top and knead them into the dough.
- Cut into ten pieces, roll each into a ball.
- Grease a baking sheet and as the balls are placed on it, slightly flatten each one.
- Cover and prove until they have again doubled in volume.
- Preheat the oven to 200°C/390°F.
- Mix the remaining egg with a few drops of water and brush over

132

the buns.
- Bake for about 20 minutes or until golden brown.
- Remove from the oven and cool on a wire rack.

PRESENTATION
- Trim the rind from the sliced cheese.
- Cut the buns in half, butter and serve with the cheese slices.

Bread for a special occasion

There are fruit breads and spice breads galore in the Dutch bakery repertoire, they are an essential ingredient of any *koffietafel* and are often eaten with a slice of cheese. One very special raisin bread is the *krentenwegge*. The birth of a baby is a time of special rejoicing and it has long been the custom in many parts of the country for the ladies of the village to get together and bake, or have baked, a very long fruit loaf – up to a metre long. This they deliver to the new mother and baby. In turn, when these ladies are invited to visit the household of the newly born, the mother offers coffee and of course, slices of the *krentenwegge*. The tradition lives on.

Oudhollandse Peperkoek – Dutch Pepper Cake

This cake is liberally 'peppered' with spices. Most of these Dutch spiced cakes are eaten spread with butter. Formerly, the recipe books would talk about sweet butter, this was just a creamy, fresh, but saltless butter which was and is the preferred type in The Netherlands for all uses; though there is excellent salted butter from the creameries. For many years if you wanted the salted variety, you bought one pound rolls of farmmade butter.

INGREDIENTS *for a 1 kg (2 lb; 4 cup) loaf tin*

375 g (12 ½ oz; 2 ½ cups) **plain flour**
1 tsp. **baking powder**
½ tsp. **each of ground cinnamon, cloves, cardamon, coriander, and ginger**
a pinch of salt
100 g (3 oz; ½ cup) **soft brown sugar**
150 g (5 fl oz; ¾ cup) **clear honey**
200 ml (7 fl oz; ¾ cup + 1 tbsp.) **milk**

PREPARATION

- Grease and flour the tin.
- Preheat the oven to 150°C/300°F.
- Sieve together the flour, baking powder, spice and salt. Add the sugar.
- Using a spoon, work in the the honey and milk until a soft dough is formed.
- Transfer to the tin and bake for 1 ½ hours.
- Remove from the tin and cool on a wire rack.

PRESENTATION

- Slice thinly and spread with butter.

Limburgse Vlaai – Limburg Flan

You may see this special Limburg dessert billed as a *Limburgse vla*, the word here has been shortened from *vlaai* which means flan. The province of Limburg is renowned for its flans, they are made with a yeast dough, sometimes open, like this one, sometimes with a latticed cover. There are not always fruit, there is a famous one with a rice filling.

The dictionary meaning of the word *vla* is 'custard'; this must be the most popular Dutch dessert, particularly with the children. Custards come readymade, fresh and long life, in several flavours, chocolate, strawberry, advocaat etc. You will find them in the stores in litre cartons, and they are a standard family dessert either singly or in combination, with or without fruit.

INGREDIENTS *for a 30 cm (12 inch) pizza type round baking tin*
For the flan
> 15 g (½ oz) **baker's yeast or 1 tsp. dried yeast**
> 100 ml (3 fl oz; scant ½ cup) **milk**
> 250 g (½ lb; 1⅔ cup) **plain flour**
> 1 tbsp. **sugar**
> ½ tsp. **salt**
> 25 g (1 oz; 2 tbsp.) **butter**

For the filling
> 750 g (1½ lbs) **summer fruit, e.g. one of the following – apples, apricots, cherries, pears or peaches**
> 100 g (3 oz; ½ cup) **granulated sugar**

PREPARATION
- Dissolve the yeast in the milk.
- Sieve the flour, sugar and salt into a bowl. Make a well in the middle and pour in the dissolved yeast, then work into a third of the flour.
- Add the butter and knead into a smooth and elastic ball.
- Cover the dough and leave until it has doubled in volume.

- Prepare the fruits. (Apples, pears and peaches should be peeled and cut into thin segments.)
- Preheat the oven to 225°C/440°F.
- Punch the air out of the dough and roll it out to fit the greased tin.
- Arrange the fruits over the dough and sprinkle with the sugar.
- Bake for 15 minutes. Cool.

PRESENTATION

- Serve at room temperature cut into wedges.

Agaricus Bisporus

Mushrooms – myths and legends behind a growing culture

Gathering fungi used to be about dawn walks in autumn woodlands or footsteps across the dew drenched fields to fill a basket with last night's crop, but these days such is the urban sprawl in western Europe that few people have the opportunity to go tracking for themselves. Perhaps it is just as well, as there are over a hundred thousand species of fungi throughout the world and certainly not all of them would go well in the family soup.

The woodland toadstool was a resting place for fairy-book elves; the fine *morel* specimen offered to the Roman Emperor Claudius by his scheming wife Agrippina, was a vehicle for poison, and in our present age those countryside 'magic mushrooms' find a ready market among a drug-hungry youth.

It is no wonder then that many western folk looked, and still look with suspicion at all mushrooms; some of the names are sinister enough to send a shiver down an ignorant spine: *Trompets de la Mort* for instance, or *Amethyst Deceiver*! Many thought that the fungi just suddenly appeared, the result of a clap of thunder in an autumn storm, as if by magic; they belonged in the world of witches and wizards, an essential ingredient in cauldrons of bubbling spells. They were the stuff of myths and old wives tales, to be found in lush green fairy rings on the garden lawn. In Ireland where I grew up, everyone knew that it was best to pick the button mushrooms as quickly as you found them, right there and then, for once you had looked at them, well for sure, they would stop growing.

We do know that man has appreciated the nutritional value of the edible fungi since the beginning of time, and for the 20th century diet-conscious cooks from the Americas to the kitchens of the Orient, they are recognized as both tasty and useful. They are low in salt, have no fat, carbohydrates, or cholesterol, but are rich in vitamins and protein.

In these western lowlands such is that intriguingly close divide between edible and poisonous mushrooms, and with so many conflicting stories on the effects of eating them, there has been a virtual taboo on them for years. It was not until as recently as the 1950s that the cultivation and marketing of the Agaricus varieties – the common whitecap button mushrooms, the *Champignon de Paris* – was seriously begun in The Netherlands. It began to happen on the farms round Horst.

In this area of north Limburg, at the heart of the fenlands called De Peel, the land is not lush or fertile. For centuries the predominantly Catholic farmers worked hard to scrape a living from the land and they were always on the lookout for new ways of increasing income in support of their numerous offspring. Mushrooms were a godsend.

A cold, moist, dark habitat is what is required, nothing special in the way of soil, just large quantities of properly rotted stuff and up they come, pushing neat and creamy-white out of the ground. Mushrooms were soon recognized as a crop which requires a minimum of space, uses quantities of compost, of which The Netherlands has always had a surfeit. Furthermore it is a crop for which the unpredictable swings of climate can be steadied by being grown under simple cover and in the early days, extensive family cooperation was able to take care of the harvesting. Eighty percent of the Dutch mushroom growers are in Limburg, North Brabant and parts of Gelderland.

The market, particularly the export market, grew beyond all expectations and The Netherlands is now in the third place on the world table of mushroom-growing countries; in Europe they are second after France.

Eating mushrooms demonstrates the variation in national tastes, even in Europe; the experimental French enjoy a wide selection, in particular the wild varieties and including those 'black diamonds' which have so far resisted the efforts of the cultivators – truffles. The cultivated 'flats' are the favourite of the English, but find no place in the Dutch market and the Germans, who eat more mushrooms than any other European nation, cannot grow enough to supply their home demand; most of the button mushrooms processed here in The Netherlands go across the border to fill the grocery shelves in Germany.

On the Dutch shopping list there has been only one kind of mushroom, the immature button, and it is only recently that a number of the wild varieties, which are now being tamed, have had a modest success in the market. Introducing new varieties locally is a slow business and farmers have been reluctant to see out the initiation period of educating their countrymen and women to try something different. The more cosmopolitan greengrocers now offer, among others, the *shiitake*, oyster and chestnut mushrooms, all under cultivation here. For the specialist kitchens there are other varieties, some imported, some dried, some tinned.

The Dutch housewife, until recently anyway, has always cooked mushrooms; either in a soup, an omelette or as a vol-au-vent filling. The pastry cases for the vol-au-vents are easy to find ready-made and of different sizes, the little ones being very much in demand over the end of the year festivities; they are usually filled with a *ragoût* of chicken, veal or mushroom; they are called *pasteitjes* and are standard fare on most snack or lunch time café menus.

Whatever kind of mushroom one prefers, the figures show that each of us here in The Netherlands eats over two kilos of fungi a year; from a slow start the numbers are rising!

An Early Autumn Dinner

~

Whether the late summer sun is still shining or the autumn
mists have closed in, we hope that this dinner with its blend
of spices and fruits will fit into either season.

Zeeduivel met een Vanille Hollandaisc
Monkfish with a Vanilla Hollandaise

Karnemelkbrood – Buttermilk Bread

~

Parelhoenfilet met een Notenkorstje
Breast of Guinea Fowl with a Nutty Crust

Spitskool met Shiitake Paddestoelen
Cabbage with Shiitake Mushrooms

Aardappelcake – Potato Cake

~

Kwetsentaart – Damson Tart

Kaneelparfait – Cinnamon Parfait

Zeeduivel met een Vanille Hollandaise
Monkfish with Vanilla Hollandaise

Our September dinner opens with a very ugly fish indeed – it sports a disproportionately large head with a ferocious set of teeth – the monkfish, also called the anglerfish, or perhaps best known by its French name *lotte*. One seldom sees the head, perhaps the fishmongers think we would be put off by its appearance! It is the tail piece that one buys, a long narrow backbone with very firm flesh; both the outer skin and the membrane covering need to be removed before cooking. Such is the texture that monkfish is sometimes likened to the meat of the lobster, and it can be served with much the same sauces one would prepare for the shellfish. It is very good for fish kebabs as it is less inclined to flake than other white fish. It has a good flavour and asks to be challenged by a sauce as distinctive as Anneke's vanilla hollandaise.

INGREDIENTS
> 500 g (1 lb) **monkfish fillets**
> **salt and freshly ground white pepper**
> 1 tbsp. **lemon juice**

For the sauce
> 100 ml (3 fl oz; scant ½ cup) **fish stock**
> ½ **vanilla pod**
> 50 ml (2 fl oz; ¼ cup) **vermouth e. g. Noilly Prat**
> 100 g (4 oz; ½ cup) **butter**
> 2 **egg yolks**
> **salt**
> **a pinch of cayenne**

> 250 g (½ lb; 1 cup) **leeks**
> 125 g (¼ lb) **large cooked shrimps**
> 1 tbsp. **butter**

- Season the fish with salt, pepper and the lemon juice.
- Put into a casserole with the stock; cover and poach for about 10 minutes or until the fish is just cooked.
- Lift the fish out with a slotted spoon, put onto a plate, cover with foil and keep warm.

- *To make the sauce:* sieve the poaching liquid into a small pan and bring to the boil with the vanilla pod and vermouth; boil until reduced to 2 tablespoonfuls.
- Melt the butter and set aside.
- Transfer the reduced liquid to a bowl, discard the vanilla pod; add the yolks and beat over hot water until thick; beat in the melted butter.
- Season with salt and cayenne. Keep warm.

- Slice the leeks thinly, wash and pat dry. Stir fry in the tablespoon of butter until soft; add the shrimps and warm through.

PRESENTATION

- Place the monkfish fillets on a warm platter. Spoon the leeks and shrimps around the fish.
- Serve the sauce separately.

Karnemelkbrood – Buttermilk Bread

Feeling thirsty? Dutch friends might offer a glass of *karnemelk* to solve that problem. In the province of Friesland it was long the custom to stand a large jug of *karnemelk* by the stove in the farmhouse kitchen for anyone who had a thirst to quench; milk, as we know it, was a luxury. The Dutch drink this smooth cultured buttermilk by the litre, as do their Nordic neighbours. It is a residue from butter and cheese making and is healthily low in fat. It is different from the more acid buttermilk we Irish use in our soda bread, for that buttermilk is rather thin and the non-pasteurized version in particular tends to separate quite quickly.

INGREDIENTS *for a 1 kg (2 lbs; 4 cup) loaf tin (for an alternative see the April recipe for cheese bread page 70)*

    30 g (1 oz) **baker's yeast or 2 tsp. dried yeast**
    300 ml (10 fl oz; 1 ¼ cups) **buttermilk**
    500 g (1 lb; 3 ⅓ cups) **flour**
    1 tsp. salt
    50 g (2 oz; 3 tbsp.) **softened butter**

PREPARATION

- Dissolve the yeast in the buttermilk.
- Sieve the flour and salt into a bowl, make a well in the middle, add the dissolved yeast and work the yeast mixture into a third of the flour.
- Add the butter.
- Knead into a smooth and elastic ball.
- Cover the dough and leave until it has doubled in volume.
- Punch the air out of the dough and form into a roll tucking in both ends.
- Transfer loaf to a greased tin and leave to prove until it has again doubled in volume.
- Preheat the oven to 200°C /390°F.
- Bake the loaf for 30 minutes.
- Remove from the tin and return to the oven, lower the oven temperature to 175°C /350°F and bake for a further 10 minutes.
- Cool on a wire rack.

Nuts

Walnuts feature in the nutty crust for this main course and it has to be said that the Dutch do know and appreciate their nuts. Most local markets will have a whole stall given over to the sale of nuts and dried fruits; they are usually unpackaged and you buy them by the *ons*, or *honderd gram* (if you are used to British measures take care, a Dutch ounce is four times heavier than a British ounce.) Nuts are considered an essential accompaniment with a *borrel* – a drink: almonds, cashew, hazelnut, peanuts are all regulars, as is a rather extraordinary mixture which goes by the name of *studentenhaver* – this consists of nuts and fruit and seems to have little connection with students!

The most important nut in this country is undoubtedly the *pinda* – peanut, probably because of the strong Indonesian influence; in fact it is not a nut at all as it grows underground and is in truth a bean. Peanut butter is a sandwich favourite and *satésaus* is a tasty dip for fried potato chips and of course as an ingredient for several Indonesian dishes (see the October chapter). There is quite a range of packed peanuts too, they come salted or unsalted, dry roasted or as *borrelnoten*, these are peanuts deep fried in batter which come in a variety of flavours. And peanuts appear at tea-time too, *pindarotsjes* – the translation is 'peanut rocks', but do not let that put you off, these are crunchy handfuls of nuts set in chocolate.

Parelhoenfilet met een Notenkorstje
Breast of Guinea Fowl with a Nutty Crust

This walnut crust is given a spicy sweet/sour twist with the addition of the chilli pepper and honey; (For information on handling chillies see page 157). This nut crust goes equally well with chicken or pork fillet.

INGREDIENTS *for 4 servings*
- 1 shallot
- 50 g (2 oz; 3 tbsp.) **butter**
- 4 **guinea fowl fillets** (approximately 125 g [4 oz] each)
- **salt and freshly ground black pepper**
- ½ a **chilli pepper**
- 100 g (2 oz; ⅔ cup) **shelled walnuts**
- 1 tsp. **honey**
- 1 **egg white**
- 250 ml (½ pt; 1 cup) **stock**
- **watercress or other garnish**

PREPARATION
- Preheat the oven to 175°c /350°F.
- Peel and chop the shallot and gently fry in half the butter in a large ovenproof casserole.
- Season the fillets with salt and pepper.
- Remove the seeds and finely slice the pepper, chop the walnuts.
- Melt the remaining butter and mix with the pepper, walnuts, honey and egg white.
- Divide the nut mixture in four and press onto the fillets to cover.
- Place the fillets in the casserole dish on top of the shallots.
- Bake uncovered for 20 minutes.
- Lift the fillets out onto a warm plate, cover with foil and keep warm.
- Add the stock to the pan juices and reduce by half over a high heat.
- Season with salt and pepper.
- Carve the cooked meat with a sharp knife, care should be taken

not to dislodge the crust; it is easier to transfer to the dinner plates if you do not carve the meat right through.

PRESENTATION

- Arrange the carved meat on the dinner plates; spoon a little of the juices around the meat and serve the rest separately.
- Decorate with a rosette of watercress.

Spitskool met Shiitake Paddestoelen
Cabbage with Shiitake Mushrooms

For this month's vegetable dish Anneke plays her part in encouraging us to use a different variety of mushroom – the oriental *shiitake*. Previously, these were only available dried but they are now cultivated in The Netherlands and their rich meaty mushroom flavour make them ideal for cooking – if putting them into a casserole it is best to add them in the last 20 minutes or so, for if overcooked they become tough. When combined with the ginger in this cabbage recipe they do lift the flavour of the leafy vegetable. There are many varieties of cabbage and in The Netherlands one would look for *spitskool* – a pointed cabbage, for this recipe.

INGREDIENTS

1 shallot
1 tbsp. butter
125 g (¼ lb) shiitake mushrooms
500 g (1 lb) cabbage
2 cm (¾ inch) fresh ginger root
salt and freshly ground black pepper

PREPARATION

- Peel and chop the shallot; in a large pan, gently fry in the butter.
- Wipe the mushrooms, slice and add to the pan. Fry for 5 minutes.
- Shred the cabbage; peel and grate the ginger, stir both into the fried mushrooms.
- Cover and turning occasionally, cook for about 15 minutes, or until the cabbage is tender but still crisp.
- Season with salt and pepper.

Aardappelcake – Potato Cake

INGREDIENTS *for a 1 kg (2 lb; 4 cup) loaf tin*

500 g (1 lb) **floury potatoes**
50 g (2 oz; 3 tbsp.) **butter**
200 ml (7 fl oz; ¾ cup + 1 tbsp.) **milk**
salt and freshly ground pepper
2 eggs
2 tbsp. grated cheese (mature)
a pinch of nutmeg
2 tbsp. dried breadcrumbs

PREPARATION

- Peel the potatoes and boil, in just enough water just to cover, until cooked; drain.
- Preheat the oven to 175°C/350°F.
- Thoroughly grease the loaf tin, sprinkle with breadcrumbs.
- Mash the potatoes with the butter and milk and season with salt and pepper.
- Mix in the eggs, cheese and nutmeg and transfer the purée to the loaf tin. Smooth the top.
- Bake for 45 minutes or until set and golden on top.
- Remove from the oven and leave for 10 minutes before turning out.

PRESENTATION

- Tranfer to a warm oval serving platter and cut into thick slices.

Kwetsentaart – Damson Tart

Damsons are a plum-like fruit, and though they are not as juicy as plums, they bake well. The rich red of the redcurrant glaze seals the surface of the tart and is well complimented by the creamy cinnamon parfait which follows this recipe.

INGREDIENTS *for a 24 cm (10 inch) loose bottomed tin*

For the pastry
75 g (2 ½ oz; ⅓ cup) **butter**
50 g (2 oz; ¼ cup) **sugar**
1 **egg**
1 tsp. grated lemon zest
150 g (5 oz; 1 cup) **plain flour**
a pinch of salt

For the filling
50 g (2 oz; ½ cup) **ground almonds**
100 g (3 oz; ½ cup) **sugar**
1 tsp. lemon juice
1 **egg**
75 g (2 ½ oz; ½ cup) **plain flour**
750 g (1 ½ lbs) **damsons**
3 tbsp. redcurrant jelly
25 g (1 oz; ⅓ cup) **flaked almonds**

PREPARATION

- *To make the pastry:* Cream the butter and sugar, beat in the egg and lemon zest.
- Sieve the flour and salt and mix into the creamed mixture to form a soft dough.
- Cover and chill for about an hour.

- *For the filling:* Mix the almonds, sugar, lemon juice, egg and flour.
- Wash, stone and quarter the damsons.
- Preheat the oven to 150°C /300°F.
- Toast the flaked almonds until golden in the oven as it warms up.

- Roll out the dough to fit the base and sides of the tin; press gently into place and trim the edges.
- Spread the almond filling over the dough.
- Cover this almond layer with the damson pieces, placing them skin side down around the dough in circles.
- Bake for 45 minutes.
- Melt the redcurrant jelly and brush over the cooked tart.

PRESENTATION
- When cool sprinkle with the toasted almonds.
- Serve with cinnamon parfait.

Kaneelparfait – Cinnamon Parfait

INGREDIENTS *for a 750 ml (1 ½ pt; 3 cup) freezer container*

250 ml (½ pt; 1 cup) **milk**
75 g (2 ½ oz; ⅓ cup) **sugar**
3 cinnamon sticks
3 egg yolks
1 tbsp. rum
250 ml (½ pt; 1 cup) **cream**

PREPARATION
- Bring the milk, sugar and cinnamon to the boil, simmer for 5 minutes.
- Mix the yolks with a little of the hot liquid; pour back into the pan and cook over a very low heat until just thickened and the custard mixture coats the back of the spoon. Do not allow to boil.
- Stir in the rum; allow to cool.
- Pour through a sieve, discard the cinnamon sticks.
- Beat the cream and fold into the cooled custard.
- Pour into the container and freeze for at least 4 hours.

PRESENTATION
- Before serving dip the container into hot water for a few seconds; turn onto a serving platter.

A Touch of Spice

East meets West in the Dutch kitchen

An exotic kaleidoscope of colours, eons of mystic legends, islands languid with the pungent scent of spices, a veritable pot-pourri of influences and cultures… this is the Indonesian archipelago; some three thousand islands topped with smoking volcanos and fringed with whispering palms. At over ten thousand kilometres from The Netherlands one could be forgiven for wondering at the inclusion of this tropical paradise in a Dutch cookbook, but the ties between these two countries, like many a marriage, 'for better or for worse' have been forged over the last 400 years. The relationship has influenced the life of both nations.

The treasures of the East first came to Europe with the Arabs and it was their traders who trekked the perilous overland routes with exotic spices for the bazaars of Constantinople. Then in the early 1500's the Portuguese fleets established a monopoly for Lisbon in the trade which was ever more in demand; and while the costs of ships and crews were becoming prohibitive, so too the profits were increasingly enticing.

Nine Amsterdam merchants certainly saw the possibilities and they signed up shareholders and crew to mount an expedition on behalf of their Far Lands Company. Their four ships sailed from The Roads off Texel in April 1595; a replica of one of those ships, The Amsterdam, lies alongside in the harbour of the capital today. This first venture was not a success however, it proved expensive in every way: many of the crew perished en route and the return on the cargo of pepper, a long fifteen months later, barely covered the expenses. They were prepared to try again and other companies followed the trail. As they met with more successful returns, so the profits from each expedition were turned round to launch the next. The competition between these independent companies was fierce and there were plenty of foreign merchants only too willing to meet demand while the Dutch squabbled at home.

It was the Dutch Republican government which in 1602 finally pressurized those groups from Amsterdam, Middelburg, Rotterdam, Delft and Hoorn to form a single United Dutch East India company – the *Verenigde Oostindische Compagnie* – commonly called the *VOC*. Over the next 200 years it went from strength to strength to become the largest trading and shipping company in the world and the Dutch ports grew prosperous on the distribution of the fragrant imports from the Orient.

Dutch tradesmen and soldiers returned to the home country from tours of duty far away with a taste for something altogether sharper and more piquant than the local fare. Spices made the merchants rich, but they also enlivened the bland northern European comestibles. It was not only the spices that found a place in the Dutch way of life, an exotic form of buffet was to be introduced by the returning officials.

Batavia, as the Dutch called their fortress city on the island of Java, and which is now part of what had been, and is again, Jakarta, grew prosperous in the 17th century. The Dutch trading men and their military protectors lived in grand style, some fine houses were built not dissimilar to those which line the canals of Amsterdam today; costly furnishings from the craftsmen of Europe were imported and mingled with the colourful batiks and finely worked ornaments of the East. The gardens were a profusion of flowering plants and tropical trees and in the market gardens, which developed in the surrounding countryside, an exciting variety of fruits and vegetables, both local and imported, grew in the rich volcanic soil. And most important of all, on the plains and on the terraced hillsides, were the paddy fields. The Indonesians have been cultivating rice for centuries; they say that the rice fields of western Java have been producing for at least two thousand years.

The local cooks educated their overseas masters from their own culinary traditions: the more subtle dishes of the Javanese, the hot spicy flavourings of the Sumatrans and the strange tropical fruits of Bali. The Arabs, Indians and Chinese too had all played their part in the background of the Indonesian cuisine, and the Dutch visitors seemed to take to them all.

It was the custom for the wealthy employees of the United East Indies Company to entertain their friends both in town and at their country seats on the cooler hills around Batavia. First to the table would come enormous platters of steamed white rice and each guest would carefully spoon a generous mound onto the middle of his plate, then with a theatrical flourish the numerous servants would re-enter the spacious dining room in single file, a serving plate held waist high in each hand. There were dishes of chicken, beef, fish, and sometimes mutton; the meats usually cut into bite size pieces and all were grilled, or stewed in rich spicy sauces with onion and garlic and coconut milk; there were bowls of soupy vegetables; and along the length of the table there were dozens of tiny bowls of hot pepper sauces and baskets of crispy prawn crackers.

Everyone helped themselves to small amounts which they heaped around the rice in such a way that the individual flavours could be tasted separately with a little of the rice. There might be upwards of 30 different offerings. The dishes would be passed again, and again. The aroma of nutmeg, cloves and ginger was rich and appetizing; the crisp vegetables a contrast to the tenderized meat dishes; spoonfuls of grated coconut cooled the *sambal* challenged palate.

In the tropical climate these hot spicy *sambals* are seen as a means to cool the body and no meal is complete without them. On the other hand, in the steamy tropical heat it is not considered important to serve the food itself piping hot.

These rice buffets gave the hostess a chance to show off her generosity with the abundance and variety of the dishes which appeared one after the other. This, then, became the basis of the *rijsttafel* as we know it today, a Dutch adaptation of an Indonesian grand meal.

For those who returned home to the Low Countries and for Indonesians who came to make their home here, the nostalgia for the spicy rice meal was no less real in the chill northerly damp and before long these needs were to be catered for. Today one does not have to walk far in any corner of this country to find an Chinees-Indisch restaurant with an amazing list of dozens of unpronounceable Indonesian dishes. Indeed until recently if I was asked what was typical about local Dutch food, with but the slightest of hesitations, I would reply: Indonesian, and then qualify by mentioning a *rijsttafel*. The restaurants make it easy by offering a set meal with anything from eight to twenty dishes, depending on your pocket as much as your hunger.

The Dutch kitchen has been enriched by contact with the far eastern islands and many of their recipes have been adopted, *nasi and bami goreng* are household names; the latter is similar to the *nasi* version but made with noodles, while *saté* – small kebabs accompanied by thick spicy peanut sauce, and *loempias* – deep fried dough packets of vegetables and meat, are on sale at every food stall. (As a teenage visitor to The Netherlands, my early memories of dinner time with my Dutch friends are of clove flavoured cabbage and cauliflower liberally sprinkled with nutmeg; very exotic flavours to someone whose only condiment had been salt and the occasional scatter of pepper.)

If you want to try some of the recipes yourself and are in search of the ingredients, most big markets in The Netherlands will have them, or try the local Toko; step inside one of these small oriental grocery stores and you will find shelves crammed high with as many herbs and spices as you could ever want and even more.

The Rijsttafel

A blend of exciting flavours as the table is laid buffet-style,
a spoon and fork for each guest and in the centre a large dish
of steaming white rice; dishes of meat and vegetables on
food warmers surround the rice; bowls of pickles and fiery
hot *sambals* complete the spread.

We wish you *salamat makan*, enjoy the touch of spice!

Nasi – Steamed White Rice

Ayam Besengek – Braised Chicken in a Spicy Coconut Sauce

Daging Semoor – Stewed Beef in a Mild Soy Sauce

Saté Babi – Pork Satay

Kuah Saté – Peanut Sauce

Sambal Goreng Telor – Eggs in a Spicy Cream Sauce

Tahu Telor – Fried Soybean Curd

Sayur Tumis Buncis – Spicy Green Beans

Acar Ketimun – Sweet and Sour Cucumber Relish

Serundeng – Spicy Coconut with Peanuts

Rujak Manis – Fresh Fruit Salad in a Spicy Palm Sugar Sauce

Eating the Indonesian way

The Indonesians really know how to enjoy their food; they seem to eat all day long. Food vendors patrol the streets and residential areas from early morning until late at night, each has a different signal – one sounds an air horn, the *saté* man makes a 'tock tock' noise with a pair of bamboo sticks and a steam whistle announces the passing by of the sticky-rice trolley.

Each proper meal is an event to be looked forward to and savoured. Traditionally, rice is eaten with every meal. The early morning *makanan pagi*, is a plate of *nasi goreng* – fried rice, this includes leftovers of meat and/or vegetables from the previous day and it may be served with strips of omelette on top. A mid morning visitor might be served a cup of sweet China tea and a piece of *kweelapis* – a spicy rice flour cake made of numerous wafer thin layers.

When the family gathers for the main meals of the day, *makanan siang* at noon, or *makanan malam* in the evening, the menu is much the same. A large platter of *nasi* – plain boiled rice, accompanied by a meat, fish or egg dish is served, plus a vegetable dish such as *gado gado* – a vegetable salad with a peanut sauce, and there will be at least one tiny dish of *sambal*.

If dessert is taken it is usually a rainbow platter of fruits: crunchy starfruit alternating with lime topped papaya; slices of succulent pineapple as a contrast to deep orange-coloured mango; or maybe whole juicy mangosteens.

Fruit juice or tea is the usual accompaniment to every meal, though the Europeans often prefer beer or tiny glasses of ice-cold geneva. And if you are being entertained Indonesian style, remember never leave an empty glass as that is considered the height of impoliteness.

A meal for four people might consist of rice plus three or four other dishes, plus side dishes: one or two varieties of *sambal*, pickles and crispy prawn crackers. The full meal given here would be very adequate for 12-14 people, though you would have to increase the quantities in some of the recipes, to

156

provide, for instance, one kebab each. As a general rule count on 75 g rice per person, 100 g meat, and 150 g vegetables.

Cooking Indonesian food, as with many of the dishes from the Far East, means careful planning and quite a lot of preparation. The cooking does not all have to be done at the last minute and indeed the flavour of many of the dishes is enhanced if made a day or so in advance.

The Indonesian cook will have four basic utensils:
a *wadjan* – this is a deep round bottomed pan, but any deep frying pan or wok will do;
a *soatil* – which is a flat wooden or metal spoon;
a *tjobeh* – instead of this mortar and pestle a small blender is a good substitute; and finally, a rice steamer, or use a heavy-bottomed pan with a tight fitting lid.

There may be some ingredients which are unfamiliar and here we give an explanation for the ones used in the following recipes, and where applicable, a substitute, though the authentic flavour is likely to be lost.
Key to names: *L*(atin), *M*(alay), *D*(utch)

Candle nut: is the oily white kernel of a nut from a Moluccan tree. The shell is broken off and the kernel toasted, the locals put them on the end of a knitting needle to roast in the oven. They are strong tasting. Substitute with almonds, Brazil nuts or macadamia nuts.
Other names: *nut of the alleurites moluccana (L), buah pelaga (M), kemiri (D)*

Chillies: there are different varieties and they can be bought fresh or dried or as a powder. There are red and green chillies and the tiny bird peppers (*chili padi*) are the fieriest. The seeds are the hottest part and you may want to remove them to reduce the heat content of the recipe. Great care should be taken when preparing chillies, some cooks even wear gloves when handling them, as even a hint of chilli on your fingers can cause a very painful reaction if you then rub your face or anywhere near your eyes.

Coconut milk: is a white creamy liquid extracted from the grated flesh of a mature coconut. Add 1/2 cup water to 1 grated coconut, knead well and

squeeze out the milk. Can be bought as a block of pure creamed coconut, or in tins. The grated flesh is not used in cooking, though finely grated and dried it is used to coat some sweetmeats. Evaporated milk could be used instead.
Other names: *santan (M), santen (D)*

Galangal: is a member of the ginger family, the root is softer and pinker than ginger, it is often called aromatic ginger. It is also sold ground, or dried, this last must be pulverized before using. If using the powdered form, then half a teaspoon is the equivalent of one teaspoon of freshly sliced. Ginger is not a substitute.
Other names: *lengkuas (M), laos (D)*

Kaffir lime leaves: these leaves come from a tree which produces a rough-skinned variety of lime which is not actually used in cooking. The leaves are usually sold dried; fresh leaves can be frozen.
A piece of lime zest could be used as a substitute.
Other names: *citrus hystrix (L), limau purut (M), djeroek poeroet/jeruk purut (D) or citrus or lime leaves*

Lemon grass: looks like a thin bamboo. The white bulbous base of the shoot can be used crushed or sliced. The stems can be sliced in half lengthwise and tied in a knot for cooking; remove before serving. It can be bought dried in which case it should be covered with hot water and allowed to stand for about 20 minutes before using. Also available in powdered form. A piece of lemon zest could be used as a substitute.
Other names: *andropogon nardus (L), sereh/serai (M), citroengras(D)*

Palm sugar: this is made from the sap of the coconut or aren palm which is boiled until it crystalizes. Sold in flat round cakes wrapped in dried leaves, to use it scrape off the required amount. Cane or soft brown sugar could be used.
Other names: *gula melaka (M), javaanse suiker, gula djawa (D)*

Prawn crackers, krupuk or *kroepoek (D)*: these are crisp crackers made from tapioca flour and often flavoured with shrimp – *kroepoek oedang (D)*; there are upwards of 25 different varieties in Indonesia.

Salam – Indonesian bay leaf – fresh and dried.

Sambal: this is a paste made from fresh chillies. It is used in cooking, but mostly as an accompaniment. It is rich in vitamin C.
There are many kinds of *sambals*, the best known are:
Sambal oelek (also called *sambal ulek)* made from ground chillies and salt,
Sambal manis: ground chillies, salt, tamarind and sugar,
Sambal terasi: ground chillies and trassi,
Sambal soy: ground chillies, shallots, lime juice, sugar and soy sauce.

Soy sauce, ketkap (D) made from soy beans. Two types: a thin watery liquid which is very salty, in Dutch *ketjap asin/zoute ketjap*, and a thicker sweeter variety, *ketjap manis/zoete ketjap.*

Tamarind: comes from a tree of the same name, the fruit forms in a pod. When fresh it is sweet tasting; you break open the pod and suck the flesh off the seed. But for cooking purposes, the ripe flesh is fermented and pressed into blocks – some with the seeds still in, or the purified variety which is clear of seeds. At this stage it is quite acid tasting, and is used as we would use vinegar, as a tenderizer. It can also be bought in a ready prepared jelly form. If unavailable use lemon juice.
Other names: *tamarindus indica (L), asam jawa (M), asem(D)*

Tofu/soy bean curd: is made from soy beans which are first boiled and then crushed, a coagulant is added to the resulting milky substance. It is drained and sold in soft blocks, similar to cheese.It can be kept for some time in the refrigerator – keep covered with water which must be changed daily. It is a rich source of protein and has a slightly nutty flavour.
Other names: *tahoe/tahu (D)*

Trassi: this is a strong dark brown paste made from salted dried shrimp; in its raw state it has a very strong, very unpleasant smell. Usually bought packaged in little squares, keep in a tightly covered jar. It must be cooked before being eaten. Ground or toasted trassi is used in very small quantities in many dishes and sambals.
Other names: *belacan (M) or belachan*

Turmeric: comes from the ginger family, the root is dried and ground; it has a bright yellow colour and has a slight fragrance. It is not a hot spice. Other names: *cuccuma longa* (L), *kunyit* (M), *koenjit* (D)

Nasi – Steamed White Rice

'Rice' to quote an Indonesian farmer, 'is a gift from the gods, the essence of life'. Legend has it that the first shoots of rice grew from the grave of the goddess Dewi Sri and even today offerings are made to her at the time of the harvest. Rice is at the heart of every Indonesian meal; it was and is the staple ingredient of that country, and is seen as a symbol of happiness and virtuosity; the amount of rice a person has in his storeroom is synonymous with his wealth and his standing in the community.

INGREDIENTS

- **300 g** (10 oz; 1½ cups) **long grain rice**
- **500 ml** (1 pint; 2 cups) **water**

PREPARATION

- Wash the rice in a colander under cold running water until the water runs clear.
- Transfer to a thick bottomed saucepan, add the water, bring to the boil and cook uncovered for 8 minutes or until the water is almost absorbed.
- Turn off heat, cover pan and leave to stand for at least 15 minutes.

PRESENTATION

- Fluff the rice with a fork and transfer to a serving bowl.

Ayam Besengek – Braised Chicken in a Spicy Coconut Sauce

(A hard nut to crack is an expression which springs to mind as I look at this recipe. I give my Dutch neighbours enormous enjoyment watching me as I stand on the front door step hurling the unfortunate coconut onto the ground, not once but several times before I manage to crack it open…) Using coconut is so much easier these days, it is no labour at all to cut a piece off a block of creamed coconut and either dissolve it in hot water to make coconut milk, or just cut it into the pot and let it dissolve with the juices or gravy.

INGREDIENTS

1 walnut size piece of tamarind
2 double chicken breasts (approximately 250 g; ½ lb each)
2 tbsp. oil
salt
25 g (1 oz; 2 tbsp.) creamed coconut
100 ml (3 fl oz; ½ cup) water
1 medium onion
2 cloves garlic
1 chilli pepper
½ tsp. trassi
2 candle nuts
1 tsp. ground cumin
1 tsp. ground coriander
½ tsp. ground galangal
1 tsp. turmeric
1 tsp. palm sugar
a blade of lemon grass
a salam leaf

PREPARATION

- Soak the tamarind in 3 tablespoons of warm water, work with your fingers to loosen the fibres; place a sieve over a container and extract as much of the liquid as possible from the tamarind pulp; reserve the liquid.
- Separate the chicken breasts and cut each fillet into 4 pieces.

- Heat the oil in a large frying pan or wok and when smoking hot fry the chicken until golden. Lift out of the oil, sprinkle with a little salt and set aside.
- Dissolve the creamed coconut in the water.
- Peel and finely chop the onion and garlic; remove the seeds from the chilli and slice; put these ingredients into a mortar with the trassi and candle nuts, then pound until you have a smooth paste.
- Mix the paste with the ground spices, grated palm sugar, and dissolved coconut.
- Pour into the frying pan; bruise the lemon grass and add with the salam leaf.
- Bring to the boil, stirring all the time.
- Reduce the heat, cover and simmer for 30 minutes.
- Add the reserved chicken pieces and heat through uncovered.
- Just before serving remove the lemon grass and salam, stir in the tamarind water and season with salt.

Daging Semoor – Stewed Beef in a Mild Soy Sauce

INGREDIENTS

    1 walnut size piece tamarind
    500 g (1 lb) stewing beef
    1 medium onion
    2 cloves garlic
    2.5 cm (1 inch) fresh ginger root
    2 tbsp. oil
    2 tbsp. sweet soy sauce
    1 salam leaf
    a pinch ground nutmeg
    salt and freshly ground black pepper

Preparation
- Soak the tamarind in 125 ml (¼ pt; ½ cup) warm water, work with your fingers to loosen the fibres; place a sieve over a container and extract as much of the liquid as possible from the tamarind pulp; reserve the liquid.
- Cut the beef into 2.5 cm (1 inch) cubes and set aside.
- Peel and finely chop the onion, garlic and ginger root; put into a mortar and pound until you have a paste.
- Heat the oil in a large frying pan or wok over medium heat; add the paste and stir-fry until golden; remove from the pan and set aside.
- Increase the heat, add the beef and fry until nicely browned.
- Add the tamarind water to the pan together with the soy sauce, the salam leaf, the nutmeg and the paste.
- Bring to the boil, reduce heat, cover and simmer very gently for about 2 hours or until the meat is very tender.
- Remove the salam before serving and season with salt and pepper.

Saté Babi – Pork Satay

The large Chinese population, which has lived in Indonesia for centuries, has incorporated into the recipes of the region many of their own ingredients, including noodles and pork; the latter forbidden by the mainly Islamic population of Indonesia. Originally most Indonesian satés were made with goat, mutton or chicken.

INGREDIENTS *for 4 satays*

300 g (10 oz) **pork tenderloin**
a clove of **garlic**
50 g (2 oz; ⅓ cup) **onion**
1 tbsp. **sweet soy sauce**
1 tsp. **lemon juice**
1 tbsp. **oil**
salt and freshly ground black pepper

PREPARATION

- Cut the meat into 1½ cm (½ inch) cubes.
- Peel and finely chop the garlic and onion and mix with the soy sauce, lemon juice and oil; season with salt and pepper.
- Add the meat. Marinade for about 30 minutes.
- Thread the meat onto skewers. If using bamboo skewers, soak them in water for half an hour before using to prevent them from burning.
- Preheat the grill; grill the meat for 3 minutes on each side.
- Serve with rice and a peanut sauce.

Kuah Saté – Peanut Sauce

The Indonesian cuisine makes extensive use of red chillies. If you are not used to eating very spicy dishes, remove the seeds before using the chillies as these are the hottest part.

INGREDIENTS

    50 g (2 oz; ⅓ cup) **onion**
    1 tbsp. **butter**
    ½ **chilli pepper**
    2 tbsp. **peanut butter**
    ¼ tsp. **trassi**
    1 tsp. **lemon juice**
    125 ml (¼ pt; ½ cup) **water**
    1 tsp. **palm sugar**
    25 g (1 oz; 2 tbsp.) **creamed coconut**
    Salt and freshly ground black pepper

PREPARATION

- Peel and finely chop the onion and fry in the butter until golden; set aside.
- Remove the seeds from the chilli pepper and chop finely.
- Mix the peanut butter with the fried onions, chilli, trassi and lemon juice.
- Put the water, sugar and creamed coconut into a small pan, heat until the sugar and coconut are dissolved. Stir into the peanut mixture.
- Season with salt and pepper.

Sambal Goreng Telor – Eggs in a Spicy Cream Sauce

There are a number of dishes which are prefixed by the word *sambal:* *sambal buncis* – spicy beans, or *sambal atie* – spicy liver; when the word is used in this way it just means peppery hot and spicy.

INGREDIENTS

- 1 walnut size piece tamarind
- 4 eggs
- 100 g (3 oz; ⅔ cup) onion
- 2 cloves garlic
- 1 cm (⅓ inch) piece of galangal root
- 1 chilli pepper
- 3 candle nuts
- ½ tsp. trassi
- 2 tbsp. oil
- 100 ml water
- 25 g (1 oz; 2 tbsp.) creamed coconut

PREPARATION

- Soak the tamarind in 3 tablespoons of warm water, work with your fingers to loosen the fibres; place a sieve over a container and extract as much of the liquid as possible from the tamarind pulp; reserve the liquid.
- Boil the eggs for 10 minutes. Peel and halve.
- Peel and finely chop the onion, garlic, galangal; remove the seeds from the chilli and slice with the candle nuts; pound all these ingredients in a mortar with the trassi until you have a paste.
- Heat the oil and when smoking hot add the paste and stir-fry for about 3 minutes.
- Add the water, tamarind liquid and the creamed coconut.
- Bring to the boil stirring constantly , lower heat and simmer uncovered for about 5 minutes.
- Put the halved eggs, cut side down, into a serving bowl, pour the sauce over them and leave to marinade for at least an hour.
- Serve at room temperature.

Tahu Telor – Fried Soybean Curd

INGREDIENTS

- 1 chilli pepper
- 3 tbsp. soy sauce
- 1 tbsp. lemon juice
- 250 g (½ lb) soybean curd
- 1 egg
- ½ tsp. salt
- 2 tbsp. oil
- 1 large onion
- 4 sprigs herb celery

PREPARATION

- Remove the seeds from the chilli and chop finely. Mix into the soy sauce with the lemon juice and add the chopped pepper.
- Cut the curd into 1½ cm (½ inch) cubes.
- Beat the egg with a fork, season with salt and pour over the curd; turn the curd carefully to coat all sides with beaten egg.
- Heat 1 tbsp of the oil in a large frying pan and fry the pieces of curd until golden. Drain and set aside.
- Chop the onion and fry in the remaining oil until golden.
- Chop the herb celery.

PRESENTATION

- Transfer the curd to a serving dish and sprinkle with the fried onion and the herb celery. Serve with the sauce.

Sayur Tumis Buncis – Spicy Green Beans

INGREDIENTS

- 300 g (10 oz) green beans
- 1 small onion
- 1 clove garlic
- 2.5 cm (1 inch) galangal root
- ½ chilli pepper

¼ tsp. trassi
2 tbsp. oil
100 g (4 oz; 1 cup) **bean sprouts**
100 ml (3 fl oz; a scant ½ cup) **water**
1 small tin/can bamboo shoots
salt and freshly ground black pepper

PREPARATION
- Trim the beans and cut into thirds.
- Peel and finely chop the onion, garlic and galangal; remove the seeds from the chilli and slice; in a mortar pound with the trassi until you have a paste.
- Heat the oil in a frying pan or wok and fry this mixture.
- Add beans and water. Bring to the boil, cover and simmer for about 15 minutes or until the beans are just tender.
- Add the bean sprouts and the bamboo shoots and warm through.
- Season with salt and pepper.

Acar Ketimun – Sweet and Sour Cucumber Relish

Even the simplest *rijsttafel* will have one or more side dishes of *atjar/acar* (D) – pickle, made from a wide variety of fruits and vegetables.

INGREDIENTS
450 g (1 lb) **cucumber**
1 tbsp. salt
1 tsp. sugar
1 tbsp. vinegar
1 chilli pepper
1 spring onion

PREPARATION
- Peel and halve the cucumber lengthwise; remove seeds if very large. Cut into thin slices, put into a colander and sprinkle with the salt; leave to drain for about 30 minutes.

- In a shallow salad bowl mix the dressing of sugar and vinegar.
- Rinse the cucumber, pressing out as much liquid as possible; put into the salad bowl; mix with the dressing.
- Remove the seeds from the chilli and cut into very thin diagonal strips; cut the spring onion into thin strips.
- Sprinkle both onto the cucumber.

Serundeng – Spicy Coconut with Peanuts

INGREDIENTS

1 walnut size piece tamarind
50 g (2 oz; ½ cup) **onion**
1 clove garlic
1 cm (⅓ inch) **galangal root**
½ tsp. trassi
2 tsp. palm sugar
1 tsp. ground coriander
½ tsp. salt
100 g (3 oz; 1 cup) **grated unsweetened coconut**
2 salam leafs
1 kaffir lime leaf
1 blade lemon grass
1 tbsp. oil
50 g (2 oz; ⅓ cup) **roasted peanuts**

PREPARATION

- Soak the tamarind in 3 tablespoons of warm water, work with your fingers to loosen the fibres; place a sieve over a container and extract as much of the liquid as possible from the tamarind pulp; reserve the liquid.
- Peel and chop the onion, garlic and galangal. Put into a mortar, add the trassi, grated palm sugar, coriander and salt. Pound until you have a paste.
- Thoroughly mix with the coconut; add the salam, kaffir lime leaf and bruised lemon grass blade.
- Heat the oil in a large frying pan or wok until hot; stir-fry the

coconut mixture over a medium heat for 5 minutes.
- Add the tamarind water and continue to stir-fry until the coconut is golden. Cool.
- Mix in the roasted peanuts.
- Stored in an airtight container it will keep for weeks.

Rujak Manis – Fresh Fruit Salad in a Spicy Palm Sugar Sauce

This is an intriguing combination of tart fruit and vegetables with the heavily flavoured palm sugar and the fiery pepper. Choose fruit which is slightly underripe and not too sweet.

INGREDIENTS

1 apple
1 pear
1 grapefruit
1 mango
250 g (½ lb) cucumber
1 chilli pepper
125 ml (¼ pt; ½ cup) water
50 g (2 oz; 1 slice) palm sugar
¼ tsp. trassi

PREPARATION

- Quarter, core and slice the apple and pear. Peel and cut the grapefruit into segments; peel and slice the mango; core and slice the cucumber.
- Remove the seeds from the chilli and chop finely.
- Put the water and palm sugar into a small pan, heat until the sugar is dissolved; stir in the chilli and the trassi and continue cooking for a couple of minutes. Cool slightly.
- Put the fruit into a serving bowl and pour the sauce over it.

One For the Pot

November – for some the month for hunting and fishing

'You are what you eat' says the poster in the doctor's waiting room, but for our ancestors the slogan might have had another twist – to be at all, you had to first catch what you would eat. Hunting, shooting and fishing are man's oldest occupations; though much discredited in some quarters today. There was a time, before supermarkets and fast food dispensers were thought of, when each household group had to provide for itself; the survivors were those best skilled at filling the cooking pot.

November in The Netherlands, as in many other parts of the northern hemisphere, was formerly the month when the butcher made his round of the farms to slaughter and prepare whatever livestock was needed to keep the farmer's family going over the long winter months. The harvest was in and it was a festive occasion enjoyed by all. The neighbours came; the men helped with the butchering, and the wives worked together salting the cuts of meat and making the sausages; there was time to exchange the news and gossip over cups of coffee or a drink. And when it was done, each of the visitors went home carrying a piece of fresh meat for dinner; for the many subsistence farm households this was a treat indeed. The larders of the nobility and the wealthy landowners were further augmented by venison and other game taken during the hunting season. Today however, there remain few tracts of land available for any but domesticated animals.

There is a small dedicated band who still tramp the Dutch fields in the short days of the year in search of game. The sport is tightly controlled; the game greatly respected; hunting is seen as a science. The hunters seek to keep a balance in the natural environment which is increasingly at risk from several interlopers. One does not have to go far in this overcrowded country to see the insidious spread of man's urban sprawl; but just as devastating is the unchecked propagation of three natural spoilers: the fox, the magpie and the crow. Take the wide expanses of the newest polder, Flevoland, within a few short years of being drained and planted, pheasants in large numbers found there a natural habitat; ten years later and they have all but disappeared, so effective has this trio been.

The huntsmen and the farmers work closely together, for where there is agricultural land there needs to be a controlled and varied range of wild and tame. The prey for the hunters is usually hare or rabbit, duck or pheasant and most of the shoots take place on farmlands.

There is one notable exception – it is a large area of mountains, drifting sand dunes and glistening fens... yes we are still in The Netherlands though perhaps I am using the geographical terms just a bit loosely as the area is only 3,300 acres and the highest mountain, the Franse Berg, is just 16 metres high! It was a private property built up initially for hunting and for that reason it was well stocked with several species of wild animal. Today, the only hunting in the park is done by the game wardens who must control the size of the thriving populations of deer and boar, and a breed of wild sheep, the horned mufflon.

The estate is the Hoge Veluwe in the far east of the country, once home to the Kröller-Müller family; it is now open to the public as a National Park and at its heart is the world famous museum which houses much of the Vincent Van Gogh collection of paintings and drawings. It was Mrs Kröller-Müller, with her deep love of art in all its forms, who oversaw the building of an extraordinarily ornate hunting lodge designed by the famous Dutch architect Berlage. Art Nouveau in style, the whole building is a symbolic reenactment of the life of the patron saint of the hunt – St. Hubertus; his misspent youth, his conversion to the more contemplative side of life, and finally the man at peace with the world around him as depicted in the rich and harmonious dining room. The concept was for a place which would be seen as a monument to both art and nature; even the sun and its seasons play a part in the mixture of light and shadow on the interior of this unique retreat for hunters.

In the present time, in the southern regions of the country there is a different group of hunters at work, employed on an important and legitimate task; they are the hawks owned by an enterprising falconer. He and his birds are much in demand and are on the job six or seven days a week for most of the year. They patrol the mussel beds of Zeeland.

The molluscs' natural habitat is in shallow tidal waterways and at the bottom of the ebb they lay themselves vulnerably bare to the sea birds that hover overhead. Gulls and oyster catchers with their sharp beaks have a gluttonous appetite for these shell fish and where better to assuage their hunger than in the rich mussel nurseries of the *Oosterschelde*. They are messy eaters and an increasing threat to the mussel industry. No man-made gadget can keep them effectively at bay, and so enter the hawks. These swooping birds of prey take out any weak or unprotected birds and effectively terrify the rest away from the mussels, in the short term anyway.

The Netherlands is very much a fishing nation, whether it be buffeting the waves in the North Sea for cod, herring or flat fish, fish farming for mussels and oysters in Zeeland, or just the lone fisherman sitting under a protective green umbrella among the reed banks of a still canal waiting for that elusive perch or pike.

Many homes in the urban areas of The Netherlands will serve a fish dish once a week; particularly in the Catholic south, where the custom was begun in the days of religious fasting. However, fish is no longer the penance it was supposed to be and it can be as expensive, if not more so, than meat. Fish farming and quick freeze technology have revolutionized the industry; salmon is now better value than cod, and while smoked fish is still popular, salt fish is almost a smell of the past. And for those who really enjoy eating fish, there are still a few restaurants where you can eat *onbeperkt scholletjes* – as many fried plaice as you can manage!

Game though is different; in the past not many Dutch family cooks would have prepared a dish of pheasant or venison for dinner, a rabbit pie perhaps on a special day. Game was both an expensive luxury and hard to find away from the countryside. Even in these days of prepared cuts of meat it is more likely that a *jachtschotel* – game casserole will be ordered from the popular November *wild menu* – game menu, on a restaurant visit. It is now possible to buy seasonal game, even in the supermarkets, but it is truly wild no more and we have to turn to the recipe makers to bring out what has become a very subdued flavour indeed.

A Game Dinner

~

Logs crackling in an open fire, the early night draws in as we
seat our guests for a seasonal meal

Salade van Zeeuwse Mosselen – Salad of Zeeland Mussels

Sesambolletjes – Sesame Rolls

~

Hazerugfilet in een Aardappelpannekoekje
Fillet of Hare in a Potato Pancake

Saus van Wintergroente – Winter Vegetable Sauce

Geglaceerde Knolraap – Glazed Swede Turnips

Stoofpeertjes – Stewed Pears

~

Appeltaartjes met Geitekaas – Apple Tarts with Goat's Cheese

Salade van Zeeuwse Mosselen – Salad of Zeeland Mussels

Traditionally, the mussels are very simply cooked in a little water with lots of chopped leeks, carrots, onions and herbs, particularly celery herb; on special occasions a dry white wine might take the place of the water. Here, although the ingredients are almost the same, we suggest an alternative mussel dish.

As mussels usually come in two kilo bags you might be wondering what to do with the other half – cook all the mussels together and chill the leftovers for frying next day; *gebakken mosselen* – mussels fried with plenty of seasoning and served on toast. *Zeekraal* – samphire or sea asparagus is an excellent accompaniment or garnish to any seafood dish, serve it raw as a garnish, or stir-fry in a little butter until just tender.

INGREDIENTS

1 kg (2 lbs) mussels in their shells
1 onion
a clove of garlic
1 carrot
1 leek
a few sprigs of herb celery
a few sprigs of parsley
1 glass of white wine
freshly ground black pepper
1 courgette (zucchini)
2 tbsp. oil
1 tsp. lime juice
2 tomatoes
25 g (1 oz) samphire

PREPARATION

- Clean the mussels under running water. Throw out any with shells that are damaged or already open.
- Peel and chop the onion, garlic, carrot and leek; put into a large pan with the herb celery, parsley, wine and black pepper.
- Bring to the boil, add the mussels. Cover the pan and boil briskly

for about 5 minutes, shaking the pan vigorously once or twice. All the mussel shells should now be open.
- Remove the mussels from their shells and set aside.
- Cut the courgette in julienne. Blanch for 1 minute in boiling salted water. Rinse under cold water and drain.
- Heat 1 tablespoon of the oil in a frying pan. Stir fry the courgette for 1 minute.
- With a slotted spoon remove from the pan and set aside.
- Peel and seed the tomatoes and cut into strips; trim the woody stems from the samphire and snip off the tender shoots.
- Heat the remaining oil and stir-fry the mussels until heated through.

PRESENTATION

- Arrange the courgette around a platter, spoon the mussels into the middle, garnish with the tomatoes and samphire and sprinkle with the lime juice; grind a little pepper over the top.
- Serve warm or at room temperature.

...And mussels alive, alive, oh...

The mussel year begins in spring among the shoaling banks of the Waddenzee off the north coast of The Netherlands. For a few short weeks, those skippers with a licence are on the hunt in this open area for the mussel seed – these are long matted clusters of young mussels who are still only a couple of centimetres long. Until recently, this was on a first come, first take-as-much-as-you-could basis and once one boat had located mussels the rest of the fleet would move in and with a great deal of barging the skippers would jostle each other in their efforts to fill the holds as quickly as possible. Today it is carried out on a much more peaceful quota system. Once loaded though, it is full throttle ahead as the trawlers steam south to their leased nursery beds in Zeeland and within hours of being lifted on board the catch is back in the sea again; a strange moment for the skippers as they see their precious cargo disappear over the side.

These young mussels will spend the next two years in their protected environment as they grow to their prime in the pure salty waters of the *Oosterschelde* – the Eastern Scheldt.

The mature mussels are finally lifted and from each trawler load a sealed bucket is taken to the auction house in the town of Yerseke, centre of the trade. Here they are inspected, measured, weighed, cooked and weighed again. The auction can begin; each prospective buyer keys in his offer; there are a couple of anxious moments round the room until the highest bidder is announced. But the mussels are not ready for the table yet, the skipper must then transport them to the buyers warehouse where they will spend the next week in enormous watertanks having a final thorough rinse through to remove any traces of sand or impurities. Then, within the span of a day, they will be lifted, moved along conveyor belts under the watchful eyes of the checkers, weighed into sacks – and then the one remaining labour intensive part of the process – sewn tightly in. Finally, they will go on sale from the market stalls in Brussels (45% of the total annual harvest), Paris (30%) or Amsterdam (20%). They are at their best in the last quarter of the year.

The mussel eating season opens with a flourish in mid August and it runs through until April. At least once during the season one or more of the towns in Zeeland has a culinary party in their market square; tressle tables fill the centre, lights and amplifiers are readied for the band, and round the edge the food stall owners light fires under huge steaming cauldrons. The menu is very simple: mussels, mussels and more mussels.

Sesambolletjes – Sesame Rolls

Sesame seeds are either white or black, there is little difference other than the visual, oh, and the price, the black are more expensive. If you cannot find sesame in your local Dutch supermarket try a healthfood shop or a Greek or middle eastern speciality store. Many breads and bread rolls in The Netherlands are liberally sprinkled with white sesame or black poppy seeds. When it comes to baking the sesame rolls, note the instruction to place them slightly apart, what you are aiming for is an attractively joined circle of rolls which can be pulled apart easily at the table.

INGREDIENTS *for 12 rolls*

15 g (½ oz) **baker's yeast or 1 tsp. dried yeast**
150 ml (5 fl oz; ½ cup + 2 tbsp.) **water**
150 g (5 oz; 1 cup) **plain flour**
½ tsp. salt
100 g (3 oz; ⅔ cup) **wholemeal flour**
1 tbsp. oil
2 tbsp. cream
1 tbsp. sesame seeds

PREPARATION

- Dissolve the yeast in the water.
- Sieve the flour and salt into a bowl, add the wholemeal flour, make a well in the middle, add the dissolved yeast and work into a third of the flour; add the oil.
- Knead into a smooth and elastic ball.
- Cover and leave until it has doubled in volume.
- Preheat the oven to 200°C /390°F.
- Punch the air out of the dough and divide into 12 pieces, form these into small rolls.
- Place the rolls on a greased baking tray, in a circle, slightly apart.
- Cover and leave to prove for a further 15 minutes.
- Brush the rolls with the cream and sprinkle with the sesame seeds.
- Bake for 15 minutes until golden brown.
- Cool on a wire rack.

Hazerugfilet in een Aardappelpannekoekje
Fillet of Hare in a Potato Pancake

Another of the 'musts' for the visitor to The Netherlands has to be a meal at a pancake house. Pancakes are a very popular dish and the restaurants seem to be in competition to see who can produce the widest choice of fillings. The most called for combination is the *pannekoek met spek en kaas* – pancake with bacon and cheese, but there are tens of possibilities both savoury and sweet, and be warned, these pancakes usually need a very large plate, so let's hope you are hungry. And to be a genuine Dutch pancake eater, dribble copious quantities of syrup over the pancake, yes even the savoury ones!

This month's potato pancakes however are quite different from those described above. When preparing the potato for the pancakes, do not rinse the grated potato even if they discolour slightly, as you need to retain as much of the starch as possible, any discolouration will disappear as you cook them and it is the starch that holds the pancake together. Note that they are only fried on one side; filled with the hare later, they will cook for another ten minutes in the oven. The pancakes can be prepared in advance.

INGREDIENTS *for 4 pancakes (each approximately 15 cm; 6 inches)*
    500 g (1 lb) waxy potatoes
    50 g (2 oz; 3 tbsp.) butter
    6 juniper berries
    1 bay leaf
    1 tsp. paprika
    1 tsp. thyme
    salt and freshly ground black pepper
    4 fillets of hare (each approximately 75 g; 3 oz)

- Cut 4 squares of greaseproof paper – large enough to hold one of the pancakes with some to spare.
- Peel and grate the potatoes.
- Divide the grated potato in four, heat a little of the butter in a frying pan; when the butter is hot add a portion of potato, pressing it gently into the butter to make a flat 15 cm (6 inch) round.
- When the underside is brown, slide onto a piece of the greaseproof paper, cooked side down.
- Bake the remaining pancakes in the same way adding more butter as necessary.
- Preheat the oven to 200°C/390°F.
- Crush the juniper berries, crumble the bay leaf and mix with the paprika, thyme, pepper and salt; rub onto the fillets.
- Place a fillet on each pancake and with the help of the greaseproof paper, close both sides of the pancake over the fillet.
- Transfer from the paper to a baking sheet, seam side down; discard the paper and bake for 10 minutes.

PRESENTATION

- Serve with the winter vegetable sauce which follows.

Saus van Wintergroente – Winter Vegetable Sauce

For the winter vegetable sauce, Anneke suggests that any full-flavoured mushroom could be used. The blackcurrant jelly has a more intense flavour than the more common redcurrant variety, and we hope that you start preparing for this recipe in the summer, as the homemade jellies are always so much nicer and not quite so sweet as the bought ones. This sauce can be made ahead of time.

INGREDIENTS

50 g (2 oz) **streaky bacon**
1 **shallot**
a **clove of garlic**
50 g (2 oz; ¼ cup) **carrot**
50 g (2 oz; ¼ cup) **celeriac**
50 g (2 oz; ¼ cup) **leek**
250 g (½ lb) **mushrooms**
2 tbsp. **butter**
250 ml (½ pt; 1 cup) **game stock**
1 tbsp. **blackcurrant jelly**
salt and freshly ground pepper
a few sprigs of parsley

PREPARATION

- Chop the bacon.
- Peel and chop the shallot, garlic, carrot and celeriac; slice and wash the leek.
- Gently fry the bacon and vegetables in the butter.
- Trim and wipe the mushrooms, cut into small pieces and add to the vegetables; continue frying for a few minutes.
- Add the stock and the blackcurrant jelly.
- Simmer for a further 10 minutes.
- Season with salt and pepper.
- Chop the parsley.

PRESENTATION

- Sprinkle the parsley on the sauce before serving.

Geglaceerde Knolraap – Glazed Swede Turnip

Swedes (or rutabaga) with their cousins the turnip have been in the 'unfashionable' basket for some years, of old they were served in Dutch homes diced, boiled and covered with a white sauce. Happily they are making a comeback with a number of new ideas for their cooking like this one which is given a bittersweet flavour by the scented kumquats.

INGREDIENTS

- 500 g (1 lb) **swede turnip**
- 6 **kumquats**
- 50 g (2 oz; ¼ cup) **butter**
- 1 tbsp. **sugar**
- 100 ml (3 fl oz; scant ½ cup) **water**
- 1 tbsp. **lemon juice**
- **salt and freshly ground pepper**

PREPARATION

- Peel the turnip and cut into thin strips, slice the kumquats.
- Melt the butter and gently fry both for about 10 minutes.
- Add the sugar and water; simmer uncovered for a further 15 minutes, stirring occasionally to prevent the vegetables sticking to the pan.
- Add the lemon juice and season with salt and pepper.

Stoofpeertjes – Stewed Pears

Stoofperen – stewed pears – are very much an autumn dish and can be bought ready cooked from the greengrocers. The red colour they seem to achieve just has to be a splash of cochineal, which in The Netherlands goes under the name *perenrood* – pear red! It was not until the end of the 16th century that the soft juicy 'beurre' pears were cultivated, before then, only cooking pears were grown. For stewing, you need to go back to these early pear varieties; in The Netherlands the best are the almost apple-shaped Brederode pears, or the smaller Gieser Wildeman.

INGREDIENTS

1 kg (2 lbs) **cooking pears**
250 ml (½ pt; 1 cup) **water**
2 tbsp. sugar
½ stick of cinnamon
a little ground cinnamon

PREPARATION

- Peel, halve and core the pears.
- Put them in a pan with the water, sugar and cinnamon stick and bring to the boil.
- Cover and simmer very gently for about 3 hours, or until the pears are soft and red/brown in colour.
- Remove the cinnamon stick.
- Lift out the pears and put in a serving dish.
- Reduce the cooking liquid until it has thickened slightly.

PRESENTATION

- Pour the reduced liquid over the pears.
- Sprinkle with a little ground cinnamon.
- Serve as accompaniment to game or meat dishes.

Appeltaartjes met Geitekaas
Apple Tartlets with Goat's Cheese

To round off the season of 'mists and mellow fruitfulness', cook these apple and cheese tartlets with spicy ginger. They are simply baked on a flat baking sheet. The choice of apples varies very much from country to country, once again, Anneke uses the Dutch Elstar as it keeps its shape.

INGREDIENTS *for 4 tartlets*

150 g (5 oz) **puff pastry (fresh or frozen)**
2 cm (¾ inch) **fresh root ginger**
2 tbsp. **butter**
1 tbsp. **honey**
250 g (½ lb) **apples (e. g. Elstar)**
150 g (5 oz) **rindless goat's cheese**
125 ml (¼ pt; ½ cup) **sour cream**
1 tbsp. **ginger syrup**
1 piece of **stem ginger**

PREPARATION

- Preheat the oven to 200°C /390°F.
- Roll out the (defrosted) pastry to a 3 mm (⅛ inch) thickness and cut out four 15 cm (6 inch) rounds.
- Place on a baking sheet which has been sprinkled with a little water.
- Peel and grate the ginger.
- Melt the butter with the honey, remove from the heat and add the grated ginger.
- Peel, core, quarter and thinly slice the apples.
- Arrange the apple in a circle on each pastry piece, slightly overlapping and leaving the centre free.
- Transfer to a baking sheet lined with greaseproof paper; brush the apples with the melted butter mixture.
- Bake the tartlets for 15 minutes, or until the pastry is golden. (These can be baked in advance.)

- Blend the cheese with the sour cream and ginger syrup; finely chop the stem ginger and stir in.
- Spoon the cheese mixture onto the centre of the tartlets and return to the oven for a few minutes, until the cheese is just beginning to melt.

PRESENTATION
- Transfer tarts to a platter and serve hot.

Sint or Santa ?

St. Nicholas or Santa Claus – or will the Dutch follow both?

His kindly face is hidden behind a long flowing beard, and astride a fine white horse he comes in the night bearing gifts and good fortune. So far, this could be one of several famed personages: Wodan perhaps, the legendary northern European figure who rode his horse across the sky during the month of December and for whom the locals left small offerings in the hopes that he would assure fertility for those homes and fields touched by his roe. But more recently in The Netherlands, the good man in question has to be St. Nicholas or *Sint* as he is affectionately called. His big day is 5th December.

We know quite a bit about St. Nicholas. He was born in Asia Minor and he was over sixty years old when he died in Myra on 6th December 343 A.D. He was a bishop with a warm generous heart and stories of his kindness spread far and wide. On one occasion, he heard tell of a family who were so poor that there could be no hope of dowries for the two daughters; the girls despaired of ever having husbands and families of their own. Touched by their sad plight, the good bishop, anonymously in the quiet of the night, dropped a bag of dowry money in each girl's shoe.

In the 15th century he was particularly revered in the city of Utrecht and on the Wadden Islands; here his faithful left small offerings for him in their shoes while they slept, hoping that he would bless their homes and farmlands. Over the years St. Nicholas has been adopted as patron saint of numerous disparate groups – merchants and prisoners, sailors and children; today you will find many churches dedicated to him, while among other great cities, Amsterdam is one which honours him as its patron saint.

Time and tradition have smudged the facts somewhat and there is no longer any religious connection with the December celebrations, although St. Nicholas continues to dress in his bishopric regalia. Towards the end of November, *Sint* arrives in The Netherlands by boat from the shores of Spain, he steps ashore on a great white horse and with him are his colourful Moorish assistants, rascally fellows, each called *Zwarte Piet* – Black Peter. They gambol along in front of the saint, throwing handfuls of sweets into the crowds and, it is believed, having an eye to the behaviour of every onlooker.

In The Hague, he lands in the fishing harbour at Scheveningen and makes his way in procession through the streets to the Spanish Embassy. From here, until the eve of his feast day, *Sint* is abroad in the cities and country alike, accompanied by his helpers; sometimes collecting notes left for him by young folk asking for some longed for plaything, and sometimes letters from grown-ups who bring him up to date on good deeds and bad. It is well known that if you sing his favourite songs loudly enough before going to bed, he just may hear and come and collect the snack you have readied for his horse, and which you have left in your biggest pair of shoes by the fireplace, or, in the modern fireless apartments, conveniently near to the front door. If you have been good, or anyway not too bad, he will fill your shoes with small presents in return.

As with many Dutch customs there is both the carrot and the stick – a reward for the good, but a threat of punishment for the bad. There is always the fear that any very naughty children will be unceremoniously packed into the empty gift sack and carted off to Spain. Small children watch the arrival of *Sint* and *Zwarte Piet* with a mixture of awed wonder and no small frisson of fear.

Then when no more excitement can be packed in, families gather on the eve of his feast, 5th December. Activity has been intense, giggles and whispers, strange objects moved to and from even stranger places. Suddenly, a heavy rat-tat-tat at the front door... the whole family falls silent... the door is opened cautiously... a black hand throws a huge handful of sweets into the hall and disappears; on the doorstep is an enormous sack overflowing with packages. What a very kind man St. Nicholas is, for even if he cannot come himself, look… each package is accompanied by a poem which explains how very well he knows every small boy or girl! It is a tense moment, as one by one the poems are read aloud but then, relief… he did read that November letter… he has brought that hoped for gift and… no… he cannot have heard of that earlier misdemeanour.

The adult members of the family put hours of preparation into their present giving; these gift 'surprises' come in many guises, nothing is what it seems, a gem might be hidden in a wobbling jelly, a handkerchief wrapped up and embedded in the bottom layer of a creamy gateau, a book pushed into the toe of a giant scarecrow, a pair of earrings concealed in the ear of a sow… the poems are even more meaningful than those for the little ones and are always anonymous. Perhaps there will be another knock at the door and a mysterious person will have left a gift on the doorstep, a teasing verse the only clue as to the donor.

There are no formal culinary traditions associated with the big day, and the only serious activity in the kitchen is likely to be in the manufacturing of a 'surprise'. Everyone will have received their own initial letter sculpted in chocolate, and *Zwarte Piet* is bound to have scattered some *strooigoed* in your direction – this mixture includes soft sugary sweetmeats and *pepernoten* – small round spicy biscuits heavily 'peppered' with ginger. Each year the confectioners dream up new ways of fashioning marzipan 'surprises' for customers to present to friends and family with those clever verses: Kermit the frog is a current favourite; the satay and chips are quite disgustingly realistic, yes… made of marzipan; and the chocolate spanner comes 'rusted' to perfection. You may be offered a *speculaaspop*, a *Sint* shaped spicy biscuit, or perhaps a piece of *boterletter*, which is an almond filled pastry, in the form of a letter, served just warm. And to round off the festivities there will be glasses of hot *bisschopswijn*, a spicy mulled wine.

These days, the people of The Netherlands are focusing more on feast of Christmas as celebrated by other nations and not a little encouraged by the mass consumerism of our age. As a Christian feast it has indeed been celebrated here, the 25th and 26th December have long been Public Holidays, but looked on as a time for serious church going, and afterwards perhaps, a meal taken with the larger family group; there is usually a tree with candles or white Christmas-tree lights but no special seasonal fare. Santa Claus is seen as a more benign visitor, one who does not bother with complicated verses and inuendos; whose helpers are more inclined to give than chastise.

What a shame it would be if the adult talk that '*Sint* is fine for the very young, but Christmas is more to our liking' were to push the Spanish based bishop into obscurity in favour of the white-bearded fellow from the North Pole.

Celebrating

～

Our December recipes are presented in two parts: first we
give you the traditional biscuits, pastries and breads
associated with the feast of St. Nicholas and Christmas in
The Netherlands, accompanied by the mulled wine so
popular at this time of year. The festive dinner comes later.

Speculaasbrokken – Spicy Biscuit Pieces

Gevulde Speculaas – Spicy Biscuits with Almond Filling

Boterletter – Almond Filled Pastry Initial

～

Kerstkransjes – Christmas Wreath Biscuits

Kerststol – Christmas Fruit Bread

Amandeltaartjes – Almond Tartlets

～

Bisschopswijn – Mulled Wine

Speculaasbrokken – Spicy Biscuit Pieces

December is the month to purchase fresh supplies of all the spices, because no matter how well they are sealed in storage jars they do lose their full flavour. For the *speculaas* you can buy ready mixed spices – *speculaaskruiden* – but for those of you not living conveniently near The Netherlands Anneke gives you the quantities of the five spices so that you can mix your own.

These biscuits are actually baked as a slab, which is then broken into pieces for serving. *Speculaas* dough can also be shaped in special moulds – *speculaasplanken,* these come in various designs including that of the Saint himself; they are handmade in wood and while they can be bought new, the old ones are much sought after as collector's items. The wooden moulds must be soaked in salted water for a few hours, wiped dry and dusted with flour before using.

Almonds play an even larger part than usual in the Dutch baking scene at this time of year. There are two varieties of almond paste, – *amandelspijs* and *marsepein* – marzipan. The first has equal amounts of almonds and granulated sugar bound together with a little egg and lemon zest to make a crunchy paste for use in baking. Some of the cheaper brands of readymade paste and of so called *gevulde* – filled pastries, use ground white beans and almond essence, so for the real thing make sure you buy from a reputable baker. Marzipan has altogether a much finer texture with a higher sugar content; it is used to fashion all the elaborate confections so popular at this time of year.

INGREDIENTS

For the speculaas dough
- **250 g** (½ lb; 1 ⅔ cups) **plain flour**
- **¼ tsp. baking powder**
- **¼ tsp. salt**
- **½ tsp. cinnamon**
- **1 tsp. ground ginger**
- **½ tsp. ground nutmeg**
- **½ tsp. ground cloves**
- **¼ tsp. ground aniseed**
- **150 g** (5 oz; ⅔ cup) **butter**
- **100 g** (3 oz; ½ cup) **soft brown sugar**
- **3 tbsp. milk**
- **20 blanched almonds**
- **1 tbsp. cream**

PREPARATION
- Sieve the flour with the baking powder, salt and all the spices.
- Cream the butter and sugar; mix in the flour and spices, adding the milk, until a soft dough is formed.
- Cover the dough and leave in a cool place for a few hours, or overnight.
- Preheat the oven to 175°C /350°F.
- Halve the almonds.
- On a greased baking sheet roll out the dough into a thick rectangle, approximately 20 × 25 cm (8 × 10 inches).
- Brush with a little cream and press the halved almonds into the dough.
- Bake for one hour.
- Remove from the oven and leave the biscuit to cool on a wire rack.

PRESENTATION
- Break into *brokken* – pieces.

Gevulde Speculaas – Spicy Biscuits with Almond Filling

INGREDIENTS *for a 20 cm (8 inch) square cake tin*
For the almond paste
    150 g (5 oz; 1 ½ cups) **ground almonds**
    125 g (4 oz; 1 ¼ cups) **icing sugar**
    1 tsp. grated lemon zest
    1 small egg

    1 recipe of *speculaas* **dough** (see previous recipe)
    1 tbsp. cream
    10 blanched almonds for decoration

PREPARATION

- Preheat oven to 175°C/350°F.
- *To make the almond paste:* Mix the ground almonds,sugar lemon zest and egg to form a stiff paste, cover and chill for at least an hour.
- *To make the speculaas dough:* See previous recipe for ingredients and preparation.
- *To assemble the speculaas:* Sprinkle a work surface with icing sugar and roll out the paste to the size of the tin, set aside.
- Divide the speculaas dough in half. Roll each half to fit the tin.
- Press one half of the dough into a greased cake tin, put the almond layer on top, then lay the remaining dough on top.
- Brush with the cream; cut the blanched almonds in half and press into the dough.
- Bake for 45 minutes at 160°C/320°F.
- Cool in the tin before turning out.

PRESENTATION

- Cut into small squares.

Boterletter – Almond Filled Pastry Initial

Another popular treat during this month is the *boterletter,* also called a *banketletter,* a rich buttery pastry filled with almond paste; for the early December festivities it comes in the shape of the letter 'S' for *Sint,* or 'M' for mother. At Christmas time a circular variety is made – *Kerstkrans,* a Christmas wreath. This pastry is brushed with a glaze – 50 g (2 oz; ½ cup) icing sugar beaten with a few drops of cold water, and decorated with glacé cherries and strips of candied orange peel.

INGREDIENTS

250 g (½ lb) **puff pastry** (fresh or frozen)
1 **recipe of almond paste** (see above)
2 tbsp. apricot jam

PREPARATION

- Roll out the (defrosted) pastry to a 10 × 60 cm (4 × 24 inch) rectangle.
- Leave to rest for 30 minutes.
- Form the almond paste into a 55 cm (22 inch) long roll.
- Place the paste roll down the middle of the pastry.
- Fold over one half of the pastry, brush with water and fold the other half on top.
- Transfer seam side down onto a baking sheet which has been sprinkled with water. Seal the ends firmly and then form into the desired letter – 'S' or 'M'.
- Loosely cover and put in a cool place to set for about 30 minutes.
- Preheat the oven to 225°C/440°F.
- Bake for 25 minutes or until the pastry is golden.
- Melt the jam and work through a sieve; brush over the hot pastry.
- Cool on a wire rack.

PRESENTATION

- Serve warm.
- To serve from cold put into a moderate oven 175°C/350°F for about 10 minutes.

Kerstkransjes – Christmas Wreath Biscuits

The *Kerstkransjes* – Christmas wreath biscuits, threaded on ribbon are a popular Christmas tree decoration. They are sprinkled with crystal sugar before baking; this sugar comes in several grades and colours, the coarse brown crystals are suitable for after dinner coffee, but for these biscuits use the slightly finer white variety, or granulated sugar.

INGREDIENTS *for approximately 50 biscuits*
- 175 g (6 oz; ¾ cup) **butter**
- 125 g (4 oz; ½ cup + 2 tbsp.) **castor sugar**
- 1 **egg**
- 250 g (½ lb; 1 ⅔ cup) **plain flour**
- 1 tsp. **grated lemon zest**
- 50 g (2 oz; ½ cup) **ground almonds**
- 2 tbsp. **cream**
- 50 g (2 oz; ¼ cup) **crystal or granulated sugar**

PREPARATION
- Cream the butter and sugar; mix in the egg.
- Sieve the flour onto the butter mixture, add the lemon zest and ground almonds and mix to form a smooth dough.
- Cover and leave to rest in a cool place for an hour.
- Preheat the oven to 180°C /360°F.
- On a floured surface roll out the dough to a 3 mm (⅛ inch) thickness.
- Using a fluted 5 cm (2 inch) biscuit cutter cut out biscuits, then with a 1 cm (½ inch) cutter, remove the centres.
- Transfer biscuits to a floured baking sheet.
- Continue in this way until all the dough has been used.
- Brush each biscuit with cream and sprinkle with the sugar.
- Bake for about 10 minutes until lightly coloured.
- Cool on a wire rack.

Kerststol – Christmas Fruit Bread

The *Kerststol*, a rich fruit bread, lists another candied fruit, citron – *sukade*, as one of the ingredients. This is a citrus fruit which when whole looks like a rough thick skinned lemon, the outer layers are candied or crystallized, the pulp is not used. Citron and ginger are used extensively in the wide variety of *ontbijtkoek* – the spicy loaves, so popular here for breakfast time all the year round. The *Kerststol* will keep very well for several weeks if completely sealed in clarified butter and sugar and wrapped securely in foil.

INGREDIENTS *for a large loaf*

250 g (½ lb; 1⅔ cups) **raisins**
100 g (3 oz; ⅔ cup) **currants**
75 g (2½ oz; ½ cup) **blanched almonds**
50 g (2 oz; ⅓ cup) **candied orange peel**
100 g (3 oz; ½ cup) **citron**
1 tsp. **grated lemon zest**
1 tbsp. **rum**
50 g (2 oz) **baker's yeast or 4 tsp. dried yeast**
50 g (2 oz; ¼ cup) **castor sugar**
250 ml (½ pt; 1 cup) **milk**
600 g (1 lb 4 oz; 4 cups) **plain flour**
1 tsp. **salt**
¼ tsp. **ground cardamon**
300 g (10 oz; 1¼ cups) **softened butter**
1 **egg**
150 g (5 oz; ¾ cup) **castor sugar**

PREPARATION

- Wash and dry the raisins and currants; chop the almonds, candied orange peel and citron; mix together with the lemon zest and rum. Cover and set aside.
- Dissolve the yeast with the sugar in the milk.
- Sieve the flour with the salt and cardamon into a large bowl, make a well in the middle, add the dissolved yeast and work into a third of the flour.

- Add 200 g (7 oz; ⅔ cup) of the butter, in small pieces; beat the egg slightly and add to the flour.
- Knead into a smooth and elastic ball.
- Cover the dough and leave until it has doubled in volume.
- Transfer to a floured surface, punch the air out of the dough and press into a rectangle; sprinkle with the fruits and nuts and knead these in.
- Roll out into a 30 × 40 cm (12 × 16 inch) oval.
- With the rolling pin mark a divide in the middle of the oval. Double over and press the edges together.
- Transfer the bread to a greased baking sheet and leave to prove for a further 30 minutes.
- Preheat the oven to 175°C/350°F.
- Bake the bread for 45-50 minutes, when cooked it should sound hollow when tapped. If the top browns too quickly while baking, loosely cover with a piece of greaseproof paper.
- Clarify the remaining 100 g (3 oz; ⅓ cup) butter by melting it gently, pour the clear liquid butter into a clean pan leaving the solids behind.
- While the bread is still warm brush all over with some of the clarified butter and sprinkle with a little of the sugar. Repeat until all the butter and sugar are used up.
- When completely cooled, wrap in foil.

PRESENTATION
- Dust with a little icing sugar.
- Serve thinly sliced, plain or spread with a little butter.

Amandeltaartjes – Almond Tartlets

For the last pastry recipe in this section I just have to quote a few lines from Cyrano de Bergerac that really sum up all these seasonal goodies:
'…melting mouths and hearts
mmmmmm… saliva starts,
Almond tarts.'
And if you are wondering what to do with the leftover egg whites from this tart recipe, you will need them for the chocolate sandwich that follows as part of the Festive Dinner. (Egg whites freeze well; put 2 or 3 whites into a small container, cover carefully and remember to mark the number of whites on each container.)

INGREDIENTS *for 12 tartlets (use a 12-hole bun sheet)*
For the pastry
120 g (4 oz; ½ cup) **butter**
60 g (2 oz; ⅓ cup) **sugar**
a pinch of salt
2 egg yolks
180 g (6 oz; 1 cup + 2 tbsp.) **plain flour**

For the filling
100 g (3 oz; 1 cup) **ground almonds**
135 g (4 ½ oz; 1 ⅓ cups) **sugar**
1 tsp. **grated lemon zest**
1 tbsp. **lemon juice**
3 **egg yolks**
25 g (1 oz; ⅓ cup) **flaked almonds**

PREPARATION
- *To make the pastry:* Cream the butter with the sugar and salt; gradually add the yolks.
- Sieve the flour over the butter mixture and mix to form a smooth dough.
- Cover and leave to rest for an hour.

- *To make the filling:* Mix the almonds with the sugar, lemon zest, lemon juice, and egg yolks until a soft paste is formed; leave to rest for 30 minutes.
- Preheat the oven to 175°C/350°F.

- *To assemble the tartlets:* On a floured surface roll out the dough to a 3 mm (⅛ inch) thickness; cut out 12 rounds to line the tartlet tins; divide the filling between the pastry cases.
- Sprinkle with the flaked almonds
- Bake for about 20 minutes or until golden brown.
- Cool before removing from the tin.

Bisschopswijn – Mulled Wine

INGREDIENTS

    1½ lt (3 pts; 6 cups) **dry red wine**
    1 **orange**
    1 **lemon**
    10 **cloves**
    ½ **cinnamon stick**
    a **blade of mace**
    2 cm (1 inch) **fresh ginger root**
    3 **cardamom pods**
    75 g (2½ oz; 1⅓ cups) **sugar**

PREPARATION

- Pour the wine into a stainless steel pan.
- Scrub the orange and lemon; stick 5 cloves into each and add to the wine with all the other ingredients.
- Cover and infuse on a hotplate for about 2 hours.
- Strain and keep warm.

PRESENTATION

- Serve in heat-resistant glasses.
- More sugar may be added to taste.

A Festive Dinner

~

This is part two of our December fare. The essence of this
festive dinner is that most of the dishes, except for the beef
and sprouts, can be cooked ahead of time so that the cooks
have time to be hosts too.

Mousse van Kippelevers met 'Tipsy' Appeltjes
Chicken Liver Mousse with Tipsy Apples

~

Langzaam Gebraden Ossehaas met een Saus van Paddestoelen
Slow Roasted Fillet of Beef with a Mushroom Sauce

Spruitjes met Spekjes – Brussels Sprouts with Crispy Bacon

Puree van Aardappelen en Knolselderij
Purée of Potatoes and Celeriac

Fruitige Cranberry Terrine – Fruity Cranberry Mould

~

Chipolata Pudding – Bavarian Cream with Candied Fruit

Chocoladesandwich met Advocaatcrème
Chocolate Advocaat Sandwich

Mousse van Kippelevers met 'Tipsy' Appeltjes
Chicken Liver Mousse with Tipsy Apples

This is a very delicately flavoured mousse. The accompanying apples should be cooked until just tender and could either be placed around the mousse or served separately.

INGREDIENTS *for a 500 g (1 pt; 2 cup) loaf tin*

For the mousse
>   250 g (½ lb) **chicken livers**
>   1 **shallot**
>   a clove of **garlic**
>   a piece **lemon peel**
>   100 ml (3 fl oz; scant ½ cup) **chicken stock**
>   1 ½ tsp. **gelatine**
>   50 g (2 oz; ¼ cup) **butter**
>   1 **egg white**
>   1 tsp. **apple liqueur**
>   **salt and freshly ground black pepper**

For the tipsy apples
>   100 ml (3 fl oz; scant ½ cup) **water**
>   50 g (2 oz; ¼ cup) **sugar**
>   a piece **lemon peel**
>   500 g (1 lb) **apples e. g. Cox's Orange**
>   3 tbsp. **apple liqueur**
>   1 **pomegranate** (optional)
>   2 tbsp. **shelled, unsalted pistachio nuts**
>   **salad greens**

PREPARATION

- *To make the mousse:* Clean the chicken livers, peel the shallot and garlic and poach in the stock with the peel for about 8 minutes. The livers should still be slightly pink.
- Remove the lemon peel; purée the liver mixture.
- In a small pan, sprinkle the gelatine over a tablespoon of water,

leave for 1 minute, then dissolve over a low heat; mix thoroughly into the purée.
- Melt the butter and add to the purée with the liqueur.
- Whisk the egg white until stiff and fold into the purée.
- Season with salt and pepper.
- Oil the loaf tin, pour in the purée, cover and chill for at least an hour, or overnight.

- *To prepare the apples:* Put the water into a medium sized pan with the sugar and lemon peel; bring to the boil and stir until the sugar is dissolved, lower the heat.
- Peel, core and cut the apples into segments, gently simmer in the syrup until the apples are just tender.
- Remove the lemon peel.
- Transfer the apples and any remaining syrup into a serving bowl, sprinkle with the liqueur. Cover and leave to cool.
- Toast and chop the pistachio nuts.
- Cut through the outside skin of the pomegranate (if used), peel back and remove the seeds with a spoon and scatter over the apples just before serving.

PRESENTATION

- Turn the mousse out onto a bed of salad greens and sprinkle with the pistachio nuts; serve with the apples.

Time for a borrel – an introduction to some very Dutch drinks

An empty tulip shaped glass is put in front of you and from a height a clear ice-cold liquid is poured up to the rim, not a drop is spilt... now it is your turn, the glass is impossible to lift, so you lower your lips and very properly take a first sip... slurp. This is the way the Dutch serve *jenever* – geneva, Dutch gin; this clear geneva, called *jonge jenever* is the preferred distilled drink in The Netherlands. It is a purer form of gin than the *oude jenever*. Both are distilled from malt wine, made from a mixture of grains, and alcohol, and to which are added, in quantities kept secret by the distillers, juniper berries (hence the name) and a wide assortment of herbs.

Korenwijn, a grain wine, is aged in oak casks and has a soft velvety taste, it too should be drunk ice cold. Are you feeling the cold? Have a glass of *Beerenberg,* this drink also has a geneva base but with a strong mix of Friesland herbs; it is a 'medicinal' favourite of the seafarers. *Vieux* is a sweet fruity brandy, good with morning coffee on a raw winter's day.

The Dutch distillers concoct a wide range of exotic liqueurs, and if you are looking for the real thing, seek out one of the few remaining, small, independent distillers. And of course there is beer, preferred to water until about 150 years ago, and by some even now. The small tumblers are first rinsed, not dried, and the resulting glass of beer has a good frothy head.

Finally, if you are in need of Dutch courage, ask for a *kopstoot* – a head butt, which is a glass of beer with a geneva chaser.

Cheers! Your health! or as they say *Op uw gezondheid.*

Langzaam Gebraden Ossehaas met een Saus van Paddestoelen
Slow Roasted Fillet of Beef with a Mushroom Sauce

The fillet is put into a cold oven and is then cooked at a low temperature for approximately 30 minutes to the 500 g (1 lb). Covering the meat after the cooking time and leaving it to rest improves the tenderness, and gives you time to finish the sauce. Use any kind of fully flavoured fresh mushroom, or you could use a dried variety like the cep, in Dutch it is called *eekhoorntjesbrood* – squirrel's bread.

INGREDIENTS

25 g (1 oz; 2 tbsp.) softened butter
500 g (1 lb) fillet of beef
salt and freshly ground black pepper

For the sauce
250 g (½ lb) mushrooms
1 small onion
a clove of garlic
25 g (1 oz; 2 tbsp.) butter
125 ml (¼ pt; ½ cup) white wine
a few drops of lemon juice
125 ml (¼ pt; ½ cup) cream
a few sprigs of parsley

PREPARATION

• Rub the butter over the fillet of beef, season with pepper and set aside.
• *To make the sauce:* Peel and finely chop the onion and garlic; gently fry in the butter for about 5 minutes.
• Wipe, trim and quarter the mushrooms, add to the onions, increase the heat and cook for a further 5 minutes.
• Add the wine and simmer until the mushrooms are soft.
• Season with salt and pepper; add the lemon juice; set aside.

- Insert a meat thermometer into the thickest part of the beef before putting into a roasting pan.
- Put the beef into a cold oven, turn the oven to 110°C/220°F.
- After 30 minutes check the thermometer, when it registers 50-55°C/120°F the meat should be nicely browned on the outside and pink inside.
- Take the meat out of the oven, remove the thermometer, season with salt and pepper, cover with foil and keep warm.
- Mix the sauce and the cream with the pan juices and simmer for a few minutes until heated through.
- Chop the parsley and add to the sauce.
- Slice the beef.

PRESENTATION
- Spoon a little sauce onto each individual plate, arrange the slices of beef on top and serve the remaining sauce separately.

Spruitjes met Spekjes – Brussels Sprouts with Crispy Bacon

Although this vegetable recipe just lists 'brussels sprouts' Anneke suggests we use the very tiny ones – in The Netherlands called *Bredase kogeltjes*. Although a little more work to prepare, they have a much more delicate taste.

INGREDIENTS
500 g (1 lb) **Brussels sprouts**
125 g (4 oz) **thinly sliced streaky bacon**
salt and freshly ground black pepper

PREPARATION
- Trim the Brussels sprouts and cook in a little water until just tender; the tiny ones take about 10 minutes.
- Drain.
- Cut the bacon into thin strips and fry until crisp.
- Add the sprouts to the bacon and warm through.
- Season with salt and pepper.

Puree van Aardappelen en Knolselderij
Purée of Potatoes and Celeriac

INGREDIENTS
500 g (1 lb) **floury potatoes**
250 g (½ lb; 1 cup) **celeriac**
100 ml (3 fl oz; scant ½ cup) **milk**
50 g (2 oz; ¼ cup) **butter**
¼ tsp. **grated nutmeg**
salt and freshly ground black pepper

PREPARATION
- Peel and quarter the potatoes; peel and slice the celeriac and put both into a large saucepan.
- Add enough water to cover. Bring to the boil, then reduce heat, cover the saucepan and simmer until soft.
- Mash the vegetables with any remaining liquid, the milk and half the butter.
- Season with nutmeg, salt and pepper.
- Transfer to an ovenproof dish, dot with the remaining butter.

PRESENTATION
- Before serving brown the top under a hot grill.

Fruitige Cranberry Terrine – Fruity Cranberry Mould

Cranberry sauce is a traditional accompaniment for those who have Thanksgiving or Christmas turkey and most of these tiny, tart berries come from the western side of the Atlantic, however if you have the opportunity to visit the islands of the Waddenzee off the north coast of The Netherlands, you will find them growing there in the wild. This cranberry salad looks particularly festive if set in a fluted *savarin* mould. Note that the recipe lists tinned pineapple – fresh pineapple will not set.

INGREDIENTS *for a 1 lt (2 pt; 4 cup) mould*

  2 tsp. gelatine
  300 ml (10 fl oz; 1 cup + 3 tbsp.) **blackcurrant juice**
  1 tbsp. **crème de cassis**
  1 tbsp. **lemon juice**
  50 g (2 oz; ¼ cup) **sugar**
  50 g (2 oz; ¼ cup) **tinned/canned pineapple chunks**
  150 g (5 oz; 1 cup) **fresh cranberries**
  125 g (4 oz; ½ cup) **celery**
  50 g (2 oz) **kumquats**
  50 g (2 oz; ⅓ cup) **walnuts**

PREPARATION

- In a small pan sprinkle the gelatine over a little of the blackcurrant juice, leave for 1 minute, then dissolve over a low heat.
- Stir the remaining blackcurrant juice, cassis, lemon juice and sugar together in a bowl until the sugar is dissolved.
- Thoroughly mix in the dissolved gelatine and leave in a cold place for about 30 minutes or until just beginning to set.
- Chop the pineapple, cranberries, celery, kumquats and walnuts and fold into the partly set jelly.
- Rinse the mould and pour in the jelly. Cover and chill until set.

PRESENTATION

- Dip the base of the mould in warm water, run a knife round the edge and turn out onto a serving platter.

Chocolate – a legacy from the Aztecs

Every month could be chocolate month in the Netherlands, but December more so than most. Each member of the family receives their initial sculpted in chocolate from the famous bishop of Myra, boxes of creamy handmade bonbons are exchanged at this the time of gifts, while steaming mugs of chocolate drink are the perfect antidote to the winter chill. But what exactly is chocolate? What is the Dutch connection?

The cocoa tree has flowers but no scent, the fruit or pod is nothing special to look at, it is about the size of a small rugby football, and with a similar texture, inside are 30-40 bitter, astringent beans. The Aztecs of South America used them for currency or compounded the fermented beans into a mysterious brew called 'chocolatl'.

The Spaniards brought the secret to Europe in the 16th century and guarded their monopoly on both the bean and the drink until the early years of the following century. Then the secret was out – and by the end of the 17th century the drinking of cocoa was popular at all levels of European society and the Dutch merchants in Amsterdam and Zeeland had become the leaders of the cocoa bean trade.

It was also a Dutchman, Van Houten, who in 1825 invented the process by which the cocoa powder was separated from cocoa mass and so the foundations were laid for the world's leading chocolate industry, the famous Dutch-process Cocoa. Another first for the Dutch came in 1907 when the first wrapped bar of chocolate went on sale – Kwatta's *Manoeuvre Chocolaad*. The wrapper had a marching soldier as its emblem, hence the name, and if you collected five 'soldiers', you could claim a free bar of chocolate. Today The Netherlands is the world's biggest exporter of processed cocoa butter, powder and chocolate.

Chipolata Pudding – Bavarian Cream with Candied Fruit

Chipolata pudding is deliciously creamy (and a note for our British readers, this chipolata has nothing to do with small sausages). *Bitterkoekjes* are a chewy bitter almond biscuit very popular in The Netherlands, but any small almond macaroons could be substituted. For a very grand occasion add some swirls of cream at the last minute and an extra sprinkle of candied fruit. It is not a bit slimming!

INGREDIENTS *for a 1 lt (2 pt; 4 cup) pudding mould*
  100 g (4 oz) *bitterkoekjes*
  4 tbsp. sweet liqueur (e.g. maraschino)

50 g (2 oz; ⅓ cup) **candied fruit: citron, orange, glacé cherries**
250 ml (½ pt; 1 cup) **milk**
75 g (2½ oz; ⅓ cup) **sugar**
2 **eggs**
2 tsp. gelatine
250 ml (½ pt; 1 cup) **cream**

PREPARATION

- Cut the biscuits into small pieces and sprinkle with the liqueur.
- Cut the candied fruit into small pieces and mix with the biscuits.

- *To make the custard:* Put all but 2 tablespoons of the milk into a pan with half the sugar and bring to the boil stirring until the sugar is dissolved.
- Separate the eggs.
- Beat the egg yolks with the remaining milk and sugar until light and creamy.
- Add a little of the hot milk, pour back into the pan and stir over low heat until the custard is thick enough to coat the back of the spoon. Do not let it boil.
- Sieve into a clean bowl and cool over iced water stirring frequently.
- In a small pan sprinkle the gelatine over 2 tablespoons of cream, leave for one minute, then dissolve over a low heat.
- Stir into the warm custard.
- Whisk the egg whites until they form soft peaks.
- Whip the cream until stiff and fold with the egg whites into the lightly set custard, cover and leave in a cool place until beginning to set.
- Rinse the pudding mould with cold water and fill with alternate layers of custard and fruit – placing the fruit a little in from the edge of the mould. Finish with a layer of custard.
- Cover and chill for 4 hours or until set.

PRESENTATION

- Unmould onto a serving platter.

Chocoladesandwich met Advocaatcrème
Chocolate Advocaat Sandwich

This dessert is a rich, moist, very chocolatey cake with a distinctive contrast of dark chocolate and yellow *Advocaat* cream. (see page 7)

INGREDIENTS *for two 22 cm (11 inch) sandwich tins*

50 g (2 oz; ⅓ cup) **plain flour**
40 g (1½ oz; ⅓ cup) **cocoa powder**
½ tsp. **ground cinnamon**
50 g (2 oz; 2 squares) **bittersweet chocolate**
1 tbsp. **strong coffee**
6 **egg whites**
150 g (5 oz; ¾ cup) **castor sugar**
1 tsp. **gelatine**
125 ml (¼ pt; ½ cup) **cream**
125 ml (¼ pt; ½ cup) *Advocaat*

PREPARATION

- Preheat the oven to 160°C / 320°F.
- Sieve the flour, cocoa powder and cinnamon.
- Break the chocolate into small pieces, put into a pan with the coffee, stir over low heat until the chocolate has melted.
- Beat egg whites until frothy, continue to beat adding the sugar little by little until stiff.
- Beat in the melted chocolate, then fold in the flour mixture.
- Grease the sandwich tins and divide the batter between them.
- Bake for 15 minutes.
- Turn the sponges out onto a wire rack; allow to cool.
- In a small pan sprinkle the gelatine over a tablespoon of water, leave for 1 minute, then dissolve over a low heat.
- Whip the cream adding the dissolved gelatine gradually; when stiff fold in the *Advocaat*.
- Sandwich the sponges with the cream, cover and chill until set.

- Dust with a little extra cocoa just before serving.

212

Titles of the photographs